In Defense
of Congress

In Defense
of Congress

Fred R. Harris
University of New Mexico

St. Martin's Press
New York

Executive editor: Don Reisman
Managing editor: Patricia Mansfield Phelan
Project editor: Erica Appel
Production supervisor: Joe Ford
Art director: Sheree Goodman
Cover design: Kay Petronio

Library of Congress Catalog Card Number: 92-62735

For information, write:
St. Martin's Press, Inc.
175 Fifth Avenue
New York, NY 10010

ISBN: 0-312-09456-6 (paperback)
      0-312-12304-3 (hardcover)

To my wife,
Margaret S. Elliston

ALSO AVAILABLE FROM ST. MARTIN'S PRESS

THE POSTREFORM CONGRESS
Roger H. Davidson

LESSONS FROM THE HILL: THE LEGISLATIVE JOURNEY
OF AN EDUCATION PROGRAM
Janet M. Martin

CONGRESS TODAY
Edward V. Schneier and Bertram Gross

LEGISLATIVE STRATEGY: SHAPING PUBLIC POLICY
Edward V. Schneier and Bertram Gross

BOOKS BY FRED R. HARRIS

Contents

Acknowledgments

I am very grateful to Don Reisman, Senior Editor at St. Martin's Press, for his valuable assistance in the preparation of this book and for suggesting it in the first place. I thank, too, Mary Hugh Lester of St. Martin's for her fine help.

I appreciate the excellent research assistance that Laura Harris gave me, as well as the good comments and suggestions of reviewers.

And my special thanks go to the Political Science Department at the University of New Mexico, which continued, as it has for so many years, to provide me a sheltered and encouraging home base while I went about my research and writing.

Prologue

Sometimes the issue of public approval of Congress can be reminiscent of the excuse that the president of a bankrupt dog food company gave when he was asked why the dog food, which the company claimed was the best in the world, had failed to sell. "Dogs don't like it!" he said.

Congress is the people's branch. Yet the polls all show that the people do not like Congress or the job it is doing.[1]

The people have a rather low regard for congressional ethics. "Please don't tell my mother I'm a politician," U.S. Representative Pat Schroeder (D., Colo.) tells audiences, "She thinks I'm a prostitute."[2] This line is always sure to get a laugh.

Nor do the people think much of Congress in general. "I'm going to give you some good news: Congress is out of session," U.S. Senator Don Nickles (R., Okla.) tells Oklahoma audiences after adjournment.[3] And, deriding congressional inefficiency, television commentator David Brinkley says, "It is widely believed in Washington that it would take Congress thirty days to make instant coffee."[4]

Yet, Congress is truly the first branch of the U.S. government. Writing the U.S. Constitution in 1787, the Founders gave most attention to Article I, which deals with Congress. They clearly meant the national legislative branch to be the heart of our governmental system. They felt that it was only natural, as James Madison was later to explain in *Federalist 51*, that in a "republican government the legislative authority, necessarily, predominates" (though Madison went on to say that the Constitution sought to check this power somewhat, principally by dividing Congress into two houses with "different modes of election"—the Senate by state legislatures and the House by the people in each state—and by giving the president a "negative," or veto).

Congress was ingeniously designed to represent the various states and the diverse population of the whole country, to deliberate on policy, and to originate national legislation and financial budgets in the public interest. Through the Senate, Congress could also confirm or reject presidential appointments to the executive and judicial branches and could ratify or reject treaties negotiated by the president with foreign countries. Congress was empowered to question executive proposals and budgets and to serve as a

1

watchdog over implementation of legislation and the spending of appropriated money.

Ours is the greatest and most powerful national legislature in the world. All U.S. presidents, at least up to Franklin Roosevelt, surely knew that well—though, like Roosevelt, some earlier presidents, such as Andrew Jackson, Abraham Lincoln, Theodore Roosevelt, and Woodrow Wilson, were unusually strong and powerful national leaders. But Woodrow Wilson, himself a political scientist and an expert on Congress before he became president, wrote in 1885 that "the predominant and controlling force, the center and source of all motive and of all regulative power, is Congress."[5]

He was right at the time. As the Founders expected, Congress effectively dominated the national government during most of the United States' history up to the 1930s. Congress made policy; presidents mostly implemented policy. But then a big—and permanent—shift of power began with the inauguration of Franklin D. Roosevelt in 1933.

The country was at that time in the midst of a terrible economic depression. Banks were failing. A lot of stockbrokers were selling apples—or jumping out of tall buildings. Unprecedented numbers of Americans were jobless. Soup lines and church kitchens extended handouts and help, but little hope.

Franklin Roosevelt convinced Americans that they had "nothing to fear but fear itself." Confidently, he promised them, and gave them, a New Deal—and it amounted to a vastly increased federal intervention in the United States' domestic, economic life. Soon, federal intervention brought work and relief to the unemployed, hot lunches to schoolchildren, subsidies to farmers, pensions to old people, regulations to business, and loans to home buyers. An alphabet soup of new federal executive department agencies boiled over and out of this cauldron of governmental invention and experimentation—WPA, FCC, SEC, TVA, and the like.

Congress, itself, was largely responsible for a shift in the balance of power between the legislative and executive branches. "Congress allowed the President to block out the main lines of legislative action, to set the timing for consideration of new policy, and for the most part, to fix even the details of the New Deal measures," political scientist James MacGregor Burns wrote of the Roosevelt era, adding that the policy alternatives at that time were never "between a comprehensive presidential program and a comprehensive congressional program," but between "a Roosevelt program [and] none at all."[6]

Maybe earlier, Americans had believed that business cycles—busts following booms, and booms following busts—were almost inevitable and divinely ordained. Maybe before, most people had agreed with the unfortunate President Herbert Hoover, who believed that, when things went bad, it was primarily the job of churches and charitable organizations, not that of the federal government, to deal with the resultant human misery. Maybe initially, too, most people had agreed with Hoover that governmental leadership in time of crisis should come from Congress, not from the president, but not anymore.

All that had changed. After Franklin Roosevelt, no president could ever again stand aside from the nation's economic problems and woes. From then on, presidents were expected to—and would—intervene, though perhaps not always wisely or well. Congress had given presidents a permanent mandate, and lasting tools, to deal with the economy, thereby greatly expanding the bureaucracy of the federal executive department and the power and discretion of the presidency.

The United States then fought in and won a great war, emerging from World War II a superpower with a massive, widely deployed standing army, navy, and air force and a colossal nuclear and missile arsenal of unimaginable destructiveness. A presidential finger—not the fingers of the 535 members of Congress—was on the button. There could only be one commander-in-chief, and that was the president of the United States. Postwar superpower status also transformed the United States' chief executive and chief of state, its own symbolic national leader, into the "leader of the free world."

Americans liked this strong presidency and grew to expect it. As one expert on the presidency wrote:

> Watergate notwithstanding, we still celebrate the gutsy, aggressive
> Presidents, even if many of them did violate the legal and
> constitutional niceties of the separation of powers. . . . Time and
> again polls indicate that what the country wants most—more than
> laws and programs—is a few courageous, tireless, assertive leaders in
> whom the people can put their faith—the type, by the way, who will
> undoubtedly dominate Congress.[7]

Between the legislative and executive branches, then, Congress grew to be more tractable than dominant. And concurrently with slippage in the relative power of Congress came a surge in the difficulty of its tasks.

For example, the population of America doubled after World War II, and thus the number of people each member of the House had to represent and speak for doubled as well. The federal government continued to swell, too, almost to bursting, and the issues Congress had to deal with grew enormously in both number and complexity. As two experts on Congress put it:

> It is sometimes easy to forget that until the 1930s the federal
> government had no income maintenance programs, not even social
> security; that, veterans excepted, there was no federal role in health
> and education until the 1960s; that such perennially controversial
> issues as foreign aid, space, environmental pollution and civil rights
> were not on the legislative agenda fifty years ago. . . . To most
> Americans, most of the time, it did not matter what the Congress did
> or did not do.[8]

The job of Congress became infinitely more complicated, its connection with the people of the country more tenuous. Congressional power waned, relative to the president's, and so did congressional popularity.

Even back in the 1940s, James MacGregor Burns had already begun to warn about congressional "stalemate and inaction" and "deadlock."[9] By the 1960s, complaints had only grown worse. U.S. Senator Joseph Clark (D., Pa.), for example, titled his 1968 book *Congress: The Sapless Branch* and declared in it:

> Congress has lost much of its capacity for prompt effective action and
> hence its ability to join the executive and the judiciary in meeting the
> challenges of the modern world. Its capacity for obstruction has,
> however, increased. In frighteningly Freudian fashion, Congress
> compensates for its inability to act creatively by exercising its
> negative power to the hilt.[10]

If anything, criticisms of Congress and its members have increased even more in recent years. There has been very little good news about individual senators and representatives: "bad checks" at the House bank and unpaid bills at the House restaurant; the "Keating Five" whose Senate campaigns collected huge sums from a savings and loan crook; sexual harassment and other offenses by members; "bloated" congressional staffs; fancy "perks" and big salary hikes for members. Of late, the news about Congress as an institution has not been good either: the "mess" the Senate made of its consideration of the Clarence Thomas nomination for the Supreme Court; the delay and difficulty experienced by both houses in acting to curb the skyrocketing federal deficits and debt; and, especially, "gridlock." Focus group sessions have shown the intensity of present citizen disquiet about Congress: strong feelings that Congress failed for so long to concentrate on serious domestic concerns, such as health care; as well as strong convictions that a majority of senators and representatives "talk past the issues," will not "level" with the American people, and rig things for their own re-election; that they are too partisan, too subservient to the powerful and moneyed interests, and not "sincerely motivated to serve the public interest."[11]

Little wonder, then, that the election year of 1992 saw such burgeoning efforts to limit congressional terms or that, as never before, candidates got themselves elected and reelected to Congress by running *against* Congress. How many congressional campaigns nowadays feature the candidate saying anything like "Send me back to Washington because I just love Congress"? How many campaign slogans resemble "Elect me to Congress and make the best even better"?

None do. "I have yet to hear one kind word, one whisper of praise, one word of sympathy for the Congress as a whole," former U.S. Senator William Proxmire (D., Wis.) once said. "Somebody ought to stand up for the Congress."[12]

That is the purpose of this book. It is a defense of Congress—along with some suggestions for improving it.

There has been an erosion in public trust in government and government institutions in general, not just in Congress.[13] Congress usually fares worse than the president, though, in measurements of public approval of institutions.[14] And the standing of Congress has been more or less poor for quite some time. Glenn Parker, for example, reviewed public opinion polls from 1939 through the 1980s and found that Congress "received more negative than positive evaluations of its performance in over 80 percent of the survey measurements of congressional popularity."[15]

However, though its standing has generally remained low, fluctuations have occurred in how Congress is rated—ups and downs.[16] In times of international crisis, for example, Americans tend to rally around their flag and government, and this rising tide of governmental approval raises all institutional ships. The popularity of Congress goes up along with the others.

On the other hand, when no international crisis exists and the economy is bad, Congress sinks back; its approval rating goes down in the polls. For example, one study found a "very strong linkage" between "confidence in Congress," confidence in other institutions, and "the general condition of the economy."[17] Also, when a lot of news surfaces about Congress, the institution's public standing suffers, probably because a great deal of such news turns out to be bad.[18]

The worst of all public approval problems for Congress, though, is the noisy and notorious traffic jam at the intersection of policy proposal and policy action—the dreaded "gridlock." *New York Times* reporter R. W. Apple, Jr., made this point well when he said on a 1993 television interview program that, for members of Congress, "It's worse to be a gridlocker today than to starve old people."[19] Similarly, political scientists Samuel C. Patterson and Gregory A. Caldeira wrote that "negative evaluations of Congress seem to issue at least partly from perceptions that the institution is slothful, slow, conflict-ridden, immobilized, and inactive."[20] So, when Congress was whipping through most of President Lyndon B. Johnson's Great Society legislation in the mid-1960s, the standing of the legislative branch soared: polls showed that two-thirds of Americans thought that Congress was doing an excellent or pretty good job. Conversely, during the protracted budget gridlock of 1990, when Congress and President George Bush were at loggerheads and missed deadline after deadline in trying to achieve a budget agreement, the popularity rating of Congress plunged to the lowest depths ever (and, incidentally, so did that of Bush).[21]

Berkeley political scientist Nelson Polsby wrote a kind of primer article on "Congress-bashing for beginners."[22] Those who attacked an unresponsive (and conservative) Congress in the late 1940s and the early 1960s, he said, were the liberals, and what their attacks and efforts helped ultimately to produce was a greatly strengthened presidency—what others were eventually to call an "imperial presidency." Later, Polsby wrote, Congress acted to redress this legislative–executive power imbalance, beginning with the Nixon administration years of the 1970s. In the process it created or expanded the legislative bureaucracy (for example, the General Accounting Office, the Congressional Research Service, the Office of Technology Assessment, and the Congressional Budget Office), doubled and redoubled personal and committee staffs, and adopted measures such as the War Powers Act and the Boland Amendment. After that, Polsby said, it was the conservatives who began to blast the resurgent (and Democratic) Congress for its frequent clashes with Republican President Bush.

Polsby made the point that legislative–executive conflict is *supposed* to exist in our separation of powers system. Whether the liberals (as they did formerly) or the conservatives (as they are doing presently) are attacking the independence of Congress, the United States ought not to alter the separation of powers system. For example, Polsby opposes both the adoption of a presidential line-item veto and limiting congressional terms.

All through the early 1990s, people almost had to take a number or get in line to be able to participate in the "Congress bashing" that had by then become so commonplace. Interestingly, however, when asked, a majority of the people who said that they did not approve of the job Congress was doing said nevertheless that they liked their *own members* of Congress.

You might think that, if you ran surveys in 435 House districts and found that a majority of those polled in each district approved of the job their own member of the House was doing, this finding would add up, nationwide, to approval of the job performance of Congress as an institution. But if you thought that, you would be wrong. It has not turned out that way.

People do approve of their own member of Congress—at least a majority of them do. For example, 1990 was the year of the long budget deadlock in Congress. Yet, that year, a Gallup poll showed that 61 percent of those surveyed expressed approval of the job their own representative was doing, while only 24 percent in that survey said that they thought Congress was doing a good job.[23] Reversing the question asked so as to measure *dis*approval of job performance, a *New York Times*/CBS News poll found that same year that, while only 30 percent gave negative ratings to "the way your representative is handling his or her job," 69 percent disapproved of "the way Congress is handling its job."[24] Two years later, in July 1992—with the House bank scandals and other problems, not a great year for Congress either—when only 20 percent of those surveyed were telling questioners from the *New York Times*/CBS News poll that they approved of the job Congress was doing, 52 percent were still saying that they approved the job performance of their own representative.[25]

Consider incumbent reelection rates, too. In 1990, for the fourth straight election, 95 percent or more of House incumbents running again were re-elected (and in that year, also, the success rate for incumbent senators seeking reelection was 97 percent).[26] In 1992, the very year in which fourteen states were adopting term limit proposals, 93 percent of House incumbents running in the general election were reelected.[27] Even discounting some of this success because of the facts that certain incumbents who may have been in trouble chose not to run, that others were beaten in the primaries, and that winning margins for incumbents declined, an observer could still agree with humorist Russell Baker, who said that the voters seemed to be "fed up with everybody's congressmen but their own."[28]

This seeming paradox—disapproving of Congress while approving of their own members of Congress—is explained by the fact that people expect different things from each. People expect their own member of Congress to be their advocate, to speak for them, to represent their interests. This *representation* function of Congress is performed by and large through its individual members. Constituents believe that their own member of Congress does a pretty good job at this (perhaps the representatives do a pretty good job of convincing constituents that they are doing a pretty good job).

On the other hand, people expect Congress to solve national problems. Solving national problems is the *lawmaking* function of Congress, and most people do not think Congress does very well at it. Sometimes, of course, the representative function (a member of Congress trying to prevent a home-district military base from being closed, for example) conflicts with the lawmaking function (Congress trying to cut the deficit, for example).

The truth is that, in both the representation and lawmaking functions, members of Congress, as individuals, and Congress itself, as an institution, are doing considerably better than they are given credit for. Let us consider this, then, as we proceed to a defense of Congress, with recommendations for how to fix it—first by looking at the members of Congress and, next, by looking at Congress as an institution.

PART I

Members of Congress

CHAPTER 1

Price, Pay, Perks, and Personnel

Voters believe that members of Congress, with their "perquisites and patronage," live "an insular existence" in "a cloistered, pampered world out of touch with the lives of their constituents." So said an article in the *Chicago Tribune*.[1]

An even meaner attack on members of Congress came in a 1992 *Money* magazine article, "What Congress Really Costs You: $2.8 Billion a Year," by Walter L. Updegrave. "The problems run much deeper than the scandals and perks you have read about," the article's subtitle declared ominously. "Indeed, no matter how extravagant and inefficient you now believe Congress is with your money, the reality is worse."[2]

Updegrave's article spawned others like it and also energized radio and television talk shows on the same theme, including an ABC News "Nightline" program, "A Look at Congressional Spending." Updegrave himself appeared on that show and continued his onslaught against members of Congress, saying, "I think the three words sum it up: pompous, pampered, and overpaid."[3] In the same vein, Forrest Sawyer, the host of the show, said that "what a lot of people are upset about is that . . . when they hear about the kind of money that [members of Congress] make, when they hear about the kind of money that their staff members make, when they hear about the privileges that they have, they feel like they're sending somebody to Washington who's living high on the hog while they're struggling just to make ends meet."

The principal criticisms of members of Congress have centered, then, on certain key themes: price, pay, perks, and personnel. The price of Congress, what it costs, is extravagant and skyrocketing. Members' pay is exorbitant. Representatives and senators enjoy lavish and unjustified privileges, or "perks." And congressional staffs are bloated and growing. These criticisms

11

are unfair. Let us begin with the charge about the extravagant and skyrocketing cost of Congress.

THE PRICE OF CONGRESS

First, the $2.8 billion annual figure used in the *Money* magazine article is "an utter distortion," as James K. Glassman, editor of the Washington newspaper, *Roll Call*, pointed out. That total "includes the budgets of titular legislative branch agencies, some of which have nothing, or little, to do with Congress itself: the Government Printing Office, the Library of Congress, the Copyright Royalty Commission, [the Botanic Garden], etc."[4]

Second, attacking congressional costs as too high is like asking a woman, "How's your husband?" She could well respond, "Compared to what?" The *Money* magazine article declared dramatically that its $2.8 billion figure for congressional costs meant that "the taxpayers' tab for running the 102nd Congress will approach $5.2 million per legislator this year." But Glassman of *Roll Call* pointed out rightly that such a statement "may be inflammatory, but it's totally meaningless. The Energy Department, for example, has a budget of about $15 billion. By *Money* magazine's reasoning, each of the top 500 executives at the Energy Department costs the taxpayers $30 million a year."[5]

Just as meaningless was the lead paragraph of a 1992 *USA Today* article kicking off a week-long series, "Capitol Cash: How the House Spends $700 Million on Itself," which proclaimed sensationally that "running the House of Representatives last year cost taxpayers $80,000 an hour—24 hours a day, 365 days a year."[6] So what? Running the U.S. Department of Labor, just one of the fourteen cabinet departments of the executive branch, cost taxpayers over twenty times that last year: $1.7 million an hour—24 hours a day, 365 days a year.

It does makes some sense to compare the cost of Congress to the rest of the federal budget. "One Congressional function is oversight over the activities of the executive branch, which has a budget 500 times as large as the legislative branch and an employment roster 150 times as large," Glassman of *Roll Call* wrote.[7] And, as he later pointed out to a television interviewer, "The federal budget is $1.4 trillion, OK, so [$2.8 billion is] 0.2 percent. You can eliminate all of Congress . . . just get rid of the whole darn thing, you'd save exactly as much as you would save if you cut the defense budget by less than one percent."[8]

We can also compare the cost of our national legislature to that of other countries. "You get what you pay for," said congressional observer Norman Ornstein of the American Enterprise Institute. "We have a $6 trillion economy, twice as large as any on earth. The amount of money that we pay for our government, including for our Congress, as a share of our net annual income, is small, compared to many other countries."[9]

Simply comparing dollar costs of Congress with those of other national legislatures is quite misleading, though, and it presents an old "apple and oranges" problem, too. For Congress, unlike the national legislatures of parliamentary systems, such as England's or Canada's, for example, is a separate, independent, coequal branch of government. Glassman, again, made this point:

> The [U.S.] legislative branch is not the 535 Members of Congress. It is an entire branch of the government—as laid out by Article I of the Constitution. This is why, for example, the United States spends 10 times as much [in dollars] on its legislature as do other countries, like Canada. Most other democracies have a parliamentary form of government [where there is a melding of the branches, with the parliament electing from its own membership the chief executive, who, together with cabinet ministers, is a member of, and dominates, the parliament]; the legislature itself has little to do but debate and rubber-stamp the actions of the executive. But the U.S. Congress has important functions. The Framers wanted it to be an actor—indeed, the primary government actor. Many partisan opponents of Congress, of course, would love to see it stripped of its funding and its power.[10]

Finally, we can compare the cost of today's Congress with that of much earlier congresses, as critics do—and notice, of course, an enormous increase (twice the rate of inflation over the last several decades, according to Walter Updegrave[11]). But that is not a very helpful comparison: back in the days when the federal government did very little, Congress did not have much to do, either, and, naturally, Congress did not cost very much then.

Cost Increases between World War II and the 1980s

It is important to look at how the size and activities of the federal government grew after World War II, as well as during the Great Society years of President Lyndon B. Johnson and the Nixon and Ford years that followed immediately thereafter. Washington, D.C.—and the United States—were quite different at the end of World War II from what they are today.[12] Airline travel was a rarity (only 10 million passenger miles traveled in 1950, compared with 39 *billion* in 1980). In the early 1950s, it took a new senator from Arkansas, for example, two nights and a day to get to Washington by train. The senator did not return again to Arkansas until the Congress adjourned for the year, which in those days was usually by the first of July. Television was more or less a novelty back then (9 percent of homes with television sets in 1950, compared with 95 percent just fifteen years later). Very few constituents ever traveled to see their member of Congress in Washington in those days. Hardly anyone back home telephoned a senator or representative, either, and even the mail from home was light.

There were no civil rights demonstrations in the country to speak of and no civil rights laws. Virtually nobody pushed in those days for legislation to protect the environment. The government paid little attention to the tragic pollution of our nation's air and water.

In 1950, the executive branch of the federal government, over which Congress was designed as a watchdog, still consisted of just eight cabinet departments, not today's fourteen. Neither the Department of Health, Education, and Welfare (1953) nor its later bifurcations, the Department of Education (1979) and the Department of Health and Human Services (1979), yet existed. Neither did the Department of Housing and Urban Development (1965), the Department of Transportation (1966), the Department of Energy (1977), nor the Department of Veteran's Affairs (1989).

Things changed, beginning in the 1960s and accelerating thereafter. The advent of rapid mass communications, a greatly increased American standard of living, much higher levels of education, and a concomitant, huge growth in American organizing and activism produced millions of citizens who were much more aware of what Congress was doing, much more attentive, and much more demanding. Federal programs—and the federal executive branch itself—mushroomed. The total federal budget, which amounted to just $35 billion in 1947, the first full peacetime year, and which was still only $80 billion ten years later in 1957, exploded to over $1 *trillion* by 1988.

It should be no surprise—and no disgrace, either—that the growth in the size, activities, and budget of the executive branch of the federal government was paralleled by similar growth in Congress. Soon, there were new congressional committees and subcommittees and greatly increased staff numbers to deal with the new issues, new programs, and new governmental agencies and departments. Legislators' schedules became increasingly packed, the pace of their work increasingly rushed. While a total of only seventy-eight roll call votes were taken in the Senate during the entire 1947 session, for example, by the late 1980s that number had increased tenfold. In addition, by then the average senator each day received 700 letters, talked on the telephone more than twenty times, and attended two or more committee and subcommittee sessions, while also sandwiching in numerous, often ambulatory, meetings with staff, constituents, lobbyists, and executive branch officials.

Recent Costs

Of course, the cost of Congress has swollen, compared with a much earlier period. The biggest increases came in the late 1960s and the first half of the 1970s, when the executive branch of government was also greatly expanding. But it is simply false to charge that such increases continue and that they are "out of control." As the Democratic Study Group of the U.S. House of Representatives documented in 1988:

> Since FY 1978, appropriations for congressional operations (including the House, Senate, and various related agencies) have actually *dropped* 3%, after accounting for inflation.
>
> Appropriations for the House are *down* 7% over this period. In contrast, funding for the Executive Branch *rose* 25%, adjusted for inflation, while funding for the Judiciary *rose* 59%.[13]

Similarly, the highly reliable *Vital Statistics on Congress 1991–1992* reported that "in the years between 1976, when Congress first approached the billion dollar threshold [in the cost of its operations], and 1990, legislative branch appropriations went up only 108 percent, while the consumer price index increased by 130 percent."[14]

More recently, after Congress had provided for itself a fiscal year 1993 spending level that in actual dollars was $1 million less than spent for that purpose the preceding year, the chair of the House Legislative Appropriations Subcommittee, Representative Vic Fazio (D., Calif.) pointed out that "between 1979's and 1993's legislative budgets, we have held the legislative branch to virtually zero growth in constant dollars."[15] In the fiscal year 1994 legislative appropriations bill, for the second year in a row, Congress provided aggregate budget authority for itself that was slightly below the previous year's level.[16] The fact is that the cost of Congress is *not* extravagant and skyrocketing, nor is congressional pay exorbitant.

CONGRESSIONAL PAY

Compared to what? There is no way to avoid facing that question again when considering the matter of congressional pay. Compared to the pay of legislators in other countries? To members' responsibilities? To the cost of living? To other jobs? In 1994, the annual salary of U.S. representatives and senators was $133,600 (with somewhat higher salaries for House and Senate leaders). And none of them was getting rich on it.

But before we get to comparison questions about congressional salaries, we have to deal with certain other questions first, just as the Founders themselves had to do. The most fundamental one is: should members of Congress receive any salary at all? Should good citizens serve in Congress as a kind of civic duty, free of charge—just like people serve a year without pay as presidents of local Rotary clubs, for example?

Serve without pay? Wouldn't that mean that only those who were rich or had other sources of income could represent us in Washington? Of course it would! Patricians John Rutledge and Charles Pinckney argued at the Constitutional Convention in *favor* of just such a system: government by the rich, in effect.[17] Fortunately, the great majority of Convention delegates disagreed with the idea that only the wealthy could be trusted to vote the public interest—on matters such as taxes and who would pay them and spending and who would benefit from it, for example.

No, of course not, most Americans would say today, we do *not* want to fix it so that only rich people can serve in Congress. Well, we could have something worse: a system in which people would agree to serve in Congress without public salaries because they expected to get paid from other sources. This possibility worried the Founders, too. When the first Senate was debating congressional pay, for example, as Senator William Maclay reported, ''[Senate President John] Adams was too impatient to [sit still]. . . . When Ellsworth said that the House of Lords in Britain had no pay, [Adams] hastily rose and said a seat [in the House of Lords] . . . was worth 60,000 pounds sterling, per annum. Ellsworth laid a trap for himself.''[18] And, it should be noted, a member of today's British House of Commons can still be on an interest group payroll, so long as that fact is disclosed.

All right, then, members of Congress ought to be paid; we agree on that. But a couple of other questions immediately arise: how much should they be paid? and who will decide? The Founders also had to wrestle with these questions. Let us take the last one first: who should set congressional salaries?

Congress should, of course, one way or another. How embarrassing for members to have to vote on their own salaries! How politically dangerous! But there is simply no way around it. Federal judges, presidents, and cabinet secretaries need not be embarrassed and do not have to worry about the political consequences when they accept pay raises. They cannot be charged with self-serving actions in this case because they do not set their own salaries. Congress does.

But members of Congress, by contrast, cannot avoid the charge of self-serving motives when their *own* salaries are raised. This problem has been a "200-year dilemma" for them.[19] Under the Constitution, only Congress can authorize and appropriate federal money. Only Congress controls the purse strings, in other words, which, of course, includes the purse out of which the salaries of members of Congress themselves have to be paid. Article I, Section 6, of the Constitution was written to declare that members of Congress "shall receive a compensation for their services, to be ascertained by law," that is, by Congress itself.

It was a power Congress ought not to have, some thought at the time, because "designing men" might purposely set their salaries too *low* in order to curry favor with their constituents and discourage qualified but nonwealthy candidates from serving. This argument was made by Representative Theodore Sedgwick, a Federalist from Massachusetts, for example, in the first session of the House of Representatives in 1789.[20] Although James Madison did not agree with Sedgwick's argument, he did believe that lodging in members of Congress the power to set their own salaries would create a natural pressure for keeping congressional pay down. Madison wrote that "legislative bodies have reduced their own wages lower rather than augmented them. The certainty of incurring the general detestation of the people will prevent abuse."[21]

Madison certainly proved to be right on one thing: the "detestation of the people" for congressional pay raises, whatever the level set. He was right on another thing, too. Although Madison did not feel that "the power of [Congress] to ascertain its own emolument . . . is likely to be abused, perhaps of all the powers granted, it is least likely to abuse," he recognized "a seeming impropriety" or "a seeming indecorum" in permitting legislators "to put their hand into the public coffers, to take out money to put in their pockets."[22] The people of the country have ever after agreed with Madison on both counts. They have detested virtually every congressional pay raise through the years, and they have frequently voiced hot resentment over the power of members of Congress to decide on their own compensation.

History of Congressional Pay

The first Congress, in 1789, set the pay for members of both houses at $6 a day (following a determined but ultimately unsuccessful effort by senators to give themselves $2 a day more, a differential supported, incidentally, by both Madison and President Washington). But when members of Congress voted in 1816 to change to an annual salary of $1,500, they "incurred almost instantly the severest rebuke ever visited on a House of Representatives," as Henry Adams wrote,[23] and nearly 60 percent of all House members— 128 out of 215 (including then Representative Daniel Webster, a proponent of the raise)—were immediately voted out of office.[24] The next Congress promptly repealed the pay law, but a little later, after the fuss had notably died down, they quietly raised the $6-a-day figure up to $8.

It was forty years until Congress voted another increase, to $3,000 annually, in 1855. Ten years later, the yearly salary was raised to $5,000, still not enough, however, to keep up with the cost of living. In 1873, Congress decided to set things right, all at once, with a 40 percent pay hike, to $7,000 annually (retroactive to the start of that Congress, two years earlier). This "Salary Grab Act," as it was immediately called, amounted to "Shameful Robbery" by senators and representatives, the *New York Times* blustered, including those who voted against the act and then accepted the increase, because "the Receiver of stolen goods is as bad as the thief," the *Times* said.[25] In the face of such vehement attacks, Congress repealed the raise the following year, but it was too late. Ninety-six Republican House members were thrown out of office in the next election because of their pay increase vote, causing House majority control to pass to the Democrats.

It was 1907 before Congress got up enough collective nerve to raise salaries again, to $7,500, and another eighteen years after that before another increase was voted, to $10,000. In the Great Depression year of 1932, members of Congress actually *lowered* their salaries by 10 percent, to $9,000. The next year, they lowered their pay by another 5 percent, before finally restoring the cuts in 1935.

Twelve years later, in 1947, salaries were raised to $12,500. They went to $22,500 eight years after that, in 1955, and, after another ten years, to $30,000, in 1965. Each of these increases was still behind the rate of inflation, but every one of them involved congressional votes and posed potential political problems for members.

Then, in 1967, members of Congress found a way, they thought, to get off the self-serving pay raise hook. That year, they included in the Postal Revenue and Federal Salary Act a provision creating an independent presidential commission to deal with congressional salaries (as well as executive and judicial salaries, all linked together). Once this Quadrennial Commission, as it came to be called, decided on raises, and these were endorsed by the President, the increases would go into effect automatically unless blocked by the vote of both houses of Congress. By this means, congressional pay was raised with little difficulty to $42,500 in 1969. But, after that, no raise came easily and without controversial votes. Congress voted partial raises sometimes, froze salaries at other times.

No raise at all came for nearly seven years after 1969; then the salary went up to only $44,600 in 1975. On the recommendation of the Quadrennial Commission, congressional pay was raised to $57,500 in 1977 and was increased a little more, to $60,662, in 1979. All these increases occurred with little public outcry. One reason was that Congress had also voted at this time to limit outside, earned income. In a practice left over from the days when serving in Congress had been considered a part-time job, many senators and representatives had continued to divide their attention between their lawmaking responsibilities and the private practice of law, for example. A good many members had also begun to collect honoraria for speeches and appearances.

In 1980, Congress rejected a pay increase, to $70,853, recommended by the Quadrennial Commission and President Jimmy Carter. After that, with periodic congressional fights over honoraria limits and over the raises themselves, member salaries were increased to $69,800 in 1983, $72,600 in 1984, $75,100 in 1985, and $77,400 in January of 1987.

In March 1987, there was considerable public opposition, including that of consumer activist Ralph Nader, when, on the recommendation of the Quadrennial Commission, congressional salaries were hiked to $89,500 without the House leadership permitting a vote on the raise by members of that body. But the 1987 public opposition was nothing compared to the political firestorm that swept the country in 1989 when the Commission proposed a huge salary jump to $135,000.[26] Never mind that the proposed 1989 increase, as the Quadrennial Commission said, would restore the purchasing power of congressional salaries to what it had been in 1969. In dollars, the raise still amounted to a 51 percent hike in pay for members and was just too much for congressional critics—including Ralph Nader and dozens of radio talk show hosts across the country—as well as, ultimately, an inflamed public, to countenance. Never mind, either, that the Quadrennial Commission had recommended that the increase go into effect only if Congress also prohibited its members from personally receiving any of the limited, but still rather large and potentially corrupting, amounts of money permitted as honoraria for speeches and appearances, mostly from interest groups and lobbyists. This reform linkage, outlawing personal income from honoraria, caused the citizen lobby Common Cause to support the proposed 1989 raise. And never mind that President Ronald Reagan had endorsed the Commission's recommendations before leaving office, or that his successor, George Bush, did so soon after being inaugurated. The public detested the proposed 1989 raise. Great numbers of citizens were especially infuriated by the prospect that members of the House, at least, might be able to duck a vote on the increase and still draw the $135,000.

Under the law creating the Quadrennial Commission, if either House *failed* to act, the recommended raise would automatically go into effect. Senators, of course, could not avoid voting on the raise. If the Senate leadership had tried to prevent the matter from coming up directly in that body, any senator could still have forced a vote on it, simply by offering a motion disapproving the increase as an amendment to any pending measure (since Senate rules permit such nongermane amendments). Many senators believed, though, that they could vote down the raise (which they ultimately did, 95 to 5) and still get it. They assumed that House Speaker Jim Wright would refuse to permit a vote in that body; he had that power under the restrictive House rules and had exercised it on the pay raise two years earlier.

Sure enough, at first, Speaker Wright did decide against allowing a House vote on the increase. Many House members, like a lot of senators, believed that they could posture against it and still enjoy the big raise. But the voters became more and more incensed by this seemingly cynical underhandedness. They clogged members' phone lines with an unheard of thousands and thousands of enraged calls and glutted congressional offices with mounds of indignant protest mail, many pieces of which contained tea bags to remind members of the Boston Tea Party. In the face of this onslaught, Speaker Wright reversed himself and permitted the House to vote. The pay raise sunk as if it had been written on lead tablets.

The 1989 controversy called into question the future political efficacy of the Quadrennial Commission pay raise system. It did not spell the end of the pay raise, itself, though. By late 1989, public opinion had cooled down enough that the House was able to pass a straightforward, bipartisan bill that gave senators and representatives (and judges and executive branch officials, too) immediate cost-of-living salary increases; a large and permanent salary increase to take effect after the 1990 elections; regular and automatic cost-of-living adjustments (COLAs) thereafter, like those provided for social security beneficiaries, for example, to keep up with inflation; and a ban on personal acceptance of honoraria.

A Senate majority could not be put together to pass the same bill in that body, however. Many senators up for reelection in 1990 believed that they had to vote against the raise for political reasons. So the salary measure was changed to apply in full only to House members; a more modest raise was approved for senators, who could continue collecting honoraria for speeches and appearances.

After the 1990 election, though, the Senate finally voted to sign on completely to the House system, with passage of the Ethics Reform Act, as it was called. This measure, among other things, provided for a large, identical pay raise for both houses (to $129,500 for that year), automatic COLAs in the future, and a prohibition against accepting honoraria personally. By 1993 members of both houses came to be earning $133,600 annually.

Cost-of-Living Adjustment

It is interesting that the automatic COLA system was similar to what Thomas Jefferson had proposed in 1783 for Virginia state legislators: salaries pegged to the average price of wheat during the preceding six years. In fact, James Madison borrowed Jefferson's plan and advanced it in the Constitutional Convention as a way to set congressional salaries. The delegates did not accept the idea, though.

Later, when Madison, as a member of the U.S. House of Representatives from Virginia in 1789, was putting together the proposed constitutional amendments that became, when ratified, the Bill of Rights, he added another in an attempt to deal with the self-serving nature of congressional control over member salaries. It stated, ''No law varying the compensation for the services of the Senators and Representatives shall take effect, until an election of Representatives shall have intervened.'' This proposed amendment was referred to the states, along with the others.

The first ten amendments, today's Bill of Rights, were all ratified by the necessary three-fourths of the states within two years. But the same was not true for the proposed congressional salary amendment.[27] By 1792, still only six states had ratified it, and the proposal was thought to be moribund. In fact, though, Congress had set no deadline for the amendment's approval (the Supreme Court was later to hold that timeliness on constitutional amendment ratification is a political matter and, thus, not challengeable in the courts.[28])

In the public furor that followed congressional approval of the 1873 ''Salary Grab Act,'' the Ohio legislature resuscitated the congressional salary amendment and became the seventh state to ratify it. Nothing further happened on the languishing amendment, though, during the next hundred years.

Then, suddenly, reaction to the 1977 congressional salary increase caused Wyoming to rediscover the measure and approve it, the eighth state to do so. Five years later, a University of Texas–Austin student, Gregory Watson, in the course of other research, happened to come across the fact that the congressional salary amendment was still pending. He decided to launch what was initially a one-man crusade to complete the measure's ratification. Watson's first success came in Maine in 1983. Five more states ratified in 1985; three, in 1986.

Conservative groups, as well as Ralph Nader's Public Citizen organization, joined the cause after the congressional pay raise of 1987, and the movement picked up steam. Additional waves of states voted ratification that year and in succeeding years. The torrid 1989 pay raise controversy resulted in even more state approvals.

Finally, on May 7, 1992, Michigan's legislature voted the decisive thirty-eighth ratification (for good measure, later the same month, New Jersey and Illinois became the thirty-ninth and fortieth states to ratify). The U.S. Archivist accepted the amendment as constitutional, and, by overwhelming votes in both Houses, Congress endorsed this action. The Twenty-seventh Amendment became a part of the Constitution more than 200 years after Madison had first proposed it. No change in congressional pay can go into effect after it is decided upon until an election for the House of Representatives has intervened.

Two dozen members of the House filed a lawsuit in the U.S. District Court in Washington, D.C., in late 1992, claiming that automatic salary COLAs for members of Congress, as well as the Quadrennial Commission device itself, violate the Twenty-seventh Amendment. Judge Stanley Sporkin rejected the claims. He ruled that both devices were constitutional, so long as a congressional election intervenes between the time a decision on a raise is made and the date it goes into effect. "Automatic annual adjustments to congressional salaries meet both the language and the spirit of the 27th Amendment," Judge Sporkin stated.

Note, though, that the automatic salary COLA has not worked to ensure that members of Congress can avoid voting on their own salaries, any more than the establishment of the Quadrennial Commission did. In March 1993, in fact, Congress was forced to vote on—and it adopted—an amendment to a general unemployment benefits bill that provided for a freeze in the congressional pay COLA for that year.[29] Still, Judge Sporkin was right in his ruling on the constitutionality of the COLA and the Quadrennial Commission. He was right, too, when he stated, "One way to maintain high-quality government is to provide our elected officials with a living wage that automatically changes to reflect changed economic conditions.''[30]

Comparison with Other Countries

Congress-bashers have charged in recent times that congressional pay is too high compared with the salaries received by the national legislators of other countries. There are three rather obvious responses to this attack. First, U.S. senators and representatives are not the highest paid lawmakers, according to a Reuters study.[31] Members of Japan's Diet are. In 1992, they enjoyed individual salaries considerably higher than those in America—$157,000 a year.

Second, if the comparison is with the salaries of members of national legislatures that have parliamentary systems, it is simply not an apt one. This point was made earlier about overall costs of the legislative branch. In a parliamentary system, such as that of the United Kingdom, for example, the parliament is not, strictly speaking, a separate branch—at least not in the sense that the U.S. Congress is.[32]

In Britain, the House of Commons elects the prime minister. The prime minister and almost all of the members of the cabinet are also members of the House of Commons (the others are members of the House of Lords). The party organization, influenced by the party leader—for example, the Conservative Party, led by the prime minister in 1994—slates party candidates for the House of Commons, and, once they are in office, the party organization can refuse to slate them for reelection if they stray from the party line too often. For this reason, among others, the House of Commons is said to be executive dominated.

Only bills proposed by the government have any real chance of serious consideration and passage in the House of Commons. Select committees, there, have no legislative jurisdiction; they are just study committees. No House of Commons committee can compel the appearance or testimony of government officials, nor, under the Official Secrets Act, find out or reveal what the government does not want disclosed. Standing committees of the House of Commons are not really permanent, or standing; they are actually *ad hoc* committees, each appointed to consider a particular bill, only *after* the measure has already been approved in principle by the whole House. Standing committees do not gather information or hold public hearings. Their job is to fill in the details of a measure already agreed to, then rubber-stamp it and report, and, afterward, dissolve. In short, as an expert on the British system has written, "the Government's domination of the legislative process is complete. Policy making has passed to the Cabinet; the Commons does little more than ratify."[33]

The U.S. Congress, on the other hand, was established by the Founders as a separate and independent branch of government, and it legislates, appropriates for, and oversees the operations of the other branches. Not surprisingly, our national legislators, full-time professionals with much greater power and responsibility, are paid more than those in most parliamentary systems.

Third, national legislators in certain other countries who do not make as much as their U.S. counterparts are allowed to earn and keep outside income from private sources. This was once true for members of our Congress, too. Into the 1970s, congressional members were fairly free to carry on outside private business, for example.

A good many members regularly practiced law then, as already noted, despite the fact that serving in Congress had long since become a full-time and year-round job. Not only did such outside activity distract members from their congressional duties, creating, according to critics, a "Tuesday to Thursday Club," as some members took off long weekends to devote to their private businesses or professions, but it also gave rise to quite serious problems of ethics and conflicts of interest. A glance, back then, at an edition of the national lawyers' directory, *Martindale-Hubbell*, would have revealed that the hometown law firms of a number of members enjoyed retainers from some of the nation's largest pharmaceutical, insurance, or oil companies. Had these companies retained the firms for legal competence or legislative influence? Who could say for sure?

Congress clamped down on private business activities, and the practice of law was eventually prohibited altogether for both senators and representatives.[34] But for a good while, another kind of large and potentially corrupting outside, earned income continued to be permitted from honoraria for speeches and appearances.[35] A number of members of Congress had always supplemented their inadequate congressional salaries with lecture fees, but, through the 1960s, the lectures were nearly always real lectures, made before groups, such as university audiences, without legislative axes to grind. That changed. Soon, many members were picking up fat honoraria checks from lobbyists, interest groups, and corporations that clearly wanted something in return— $2,000 for touring a company plant or mine; an all-expense-paid trip to the Bahamas for a member of Congress and his or her whole family, as well as a $1,500 speaking fee for addressing a corporate conference there; or $1,000 for simply showing up at a breakfast meeting with a certain interest group's officials.

These honoraria, for the most part, were not paid because the recipient members of Congress were known for being world-class companions, nor were they paid because the members were notably among the nation's most spellbinding and entertaining orators. Instead, the money was clearly intended to buy access and influence. For it was true then, as always, that whoever pays the piper wants to call the tune.

Congress eventually limited honoraria in two ways, with some changes from time to time: a cap on the fee permitted for a single speech or appearance, most of the time $2,000, and a cap on the total permitted to be kept from honoraria received, usually a percentage of salary, with a higher percentage allowed for senators than representatives. The amount allowed in 1988, for example, was 40 percent of their salaries for senators, and 30 percent for representatives, which amounted to $34,900 and $25,880, respectively. Senators and House members could collect honoraria in total amounts above these limits, so long as they gave the excess to charity, contributions that were frequently used to help their standings back home.

Pete Domenici, a Republican from New Mexico, was in the 1980s— and is—a fine and effective member of the U.S. Senate. He was not a person of much wealth or means. But he had a large family to feed, house, and educate, while maintaining two homes, one in Washington and one in New Mexico, and he surely could not do all this on the Senate salary of that time. His 1986 total receipts from honoraria of $78,290, of which he kept personally a little over $30,000, was about average for senators that year, and the sources of the fees he received included tobacco, power, and oil companies.

In 1990, the receipt of honoraria was prohibited altogether for representatives, and the Senate reduced the limit its members could keep to 27 percent of their salaries, or $26,568. In 1991, acceptance of honoraria was finally banned altogether for members of both houses. This ban was part of a compensation system that was designed to pay senators and representatives for their full attention to congressional duties and that, unlike the compensation systems of some other national legislatures, was intended to eliminate the need for any outside, earned income.

U.S. congressional salaries are not out of line, then, with those paid in other countries.

Salaries and Congressional Responsibilities

Neither are salaries out of line with congressional responsibilities. Cokie Roberts is a news analyst for National Public Radio and ABC News whose mother and father—Lindy Boggs and the late Hale Boggs—both served in the U.S. House of Representatives. She believes that members of Congress should be respected as career professionals and has written:

> We demand professional doctors, and we respect the practice of medicine. We expect professional bridge builders and respect the art of engineering. To say that we want only nonprofessionals governing us is to show a basic disrespect for government, and though that sentiment is popular, it is dangerous. We have nothing binding us together as a nation—no common ethnicity, history, religion or even language—except the Constitution and the institutions it created. The very glue of our nationhood rests with the judiciary, executive and especially the first branch, Congress. It is a place to be taken seriously, a place for professionals.[36]

Political scientist and congressional expert Nelson Polsby agreed with Roberts, and he emphasized the point that serving in Congress "is a job, requiring skill and dedication to be done properly. Moreover, membership in Congress brings responsibilities. National policy of the scope and scale now encompassed by acts of the federal government requires responsible, dedicated legislators."[37]

In defending Congress against what he called Ralph Nader's 1989 "completely off-the-wall effort, temporarily successful, at the head of a crazed phalanx of self-righteous disk jockeys and talk-show hosts, to deprive Congress of a salary increase," Polsby wrote that the job of a member of Congress is neither simple nor quickly and easily mastered, adding:

> The job of a member of Congress is varied and complex. It includes:
> 1. Managing a small group of offices that attempt on request to assist distressed constituents, state and local governments, and enterprises in the home district that may have business with the federal government. This ombudsman function gives members an opportunity to monitor the performance of the government in its dealings with citizens and can serve to identify areas of general need.
> 2. Serving on committees that oversee the executive-branch activity on a broad spectrum of subjects (such as immigration, copyright protection, telecommunications, or health policy) and that undertake to frame issues of national scope for legislative action. This entails mastering complicated subject

matter; working with staff members, expert outsiders, and colleagues to build coalitions; understanding justifications; and answering objections.

3. Participating in general legislative work. Members have to vote on everything, not merely on the work of their committees. They have to inform themselves of the merits of the bills, and stand ready to cooperate with colleagues whose support they will need to advance their proposals.

4. Keeping track of their own political business. This means watching over and occasionally participating in politics of their own states and localities, and mending fences with interest groups, friends and neighbors, backers, political rivals, and allies.

5. Educating all the varied people with whom they come in contact about issues that are high on the agenda and about reasonable expectations of performance. This includes the government, the Congress, and the member.[38]

That the job of a member of Congress is not an easy one is a point also made by Edward V. Schneier and Bertram Gross, in their excellent college textbook, *Congress Today:*

The typical MC [member of Congress] works sixty hours a week; like a doctor, he or she is always on call. Constituents expect him to be available, sympathetic, and interested in their problems. Colleagues expect her to be well-informed. Lobbyists expect him to listen. Journalists expect her to provide quotable comments on everything from the state of the nation to the prowess of the State University's football team.

It is impossible to present a "typical" schedule of a senator or representative, in part because the priorities of individual legislators differ, in part because one day on Capitol Hill is seldom like another. To look at an individual schedule, or to examine figures on allocations of time, is to be struck by the range and diversity of activities packed into a single day. "Members," as one study concluded, "are extraordinarily busy people. An average day for legislators is so filled with diverse activities that little time is available for concentrated attention on a single issue." A lot of work is done on the fly, walking from a hearing room to the office, the office to the floor, or on the plane back to the district. Only about three of the eleven hours a day are spent in member offices. It is not a job for a sedentary or contemplative person.[39]

Comparison with Other Professions

Most Americans find no fault today with those members of Congress who in 1816 argued that the salaries for senators and representatives ought not to be kept so low that members would be required to live "as in a boarding house, or in a monastery" or to eat "hominy and molasses in a hovel" nor held to a level sufficient only "to tempt the cupidity and excite the avarice of the second and third rate county court lawyer."[40] Today's senators and representatives are skilled and hard-working professionals, and they are entitled to the pay of professionals. Their 1994 $133,600 annual salary is commensurate to their difficult and strenuous jobs and prodigious responsibilities. The salary is commensurate, as well, to a member's cost of living and the burden for most of having to maintain homes in two places. Congressional pay is also in line with the salaries of other positions of comparable importance and duties. Consider that the annual salary of $135,000 recommended in 1989 by the Quadrennial Commission was intended to compensate for inflation during the preceding twenty years and to match the purchasing power of congressional salaries in 1969. Consider, too, that had that 1989 raise gone into effect, together with regular cost-of-living increases thereafter, members of Congress would now surely be earning in excess of $150,000 annually.

A state governor, a university president, or a corporate CEO each get to live in the same place where their main office and work are located. That is conspicuously not the case for senators and representatives. Soon after their electoral victories, members of Congress must leave for Washington in order to take office and do the job for which they were elected. This situation makes for a hectic, divided existence. It also frequently spells political trouble. Members return—virtually *must* return—to their constituencies an average of two weekends a month and spend longer periods there during summer and other breaks. And spouses have to be seen regularly among the constituents, too, even though they receive no travel and expense allowance (the members themselves receive a generous allowance).

Still, before long, Washington inevitably becomes home for most members, the former home often comes to be thought of as "the district" or "the state," and members and their families must constantly be on guard against slipping up and saying so in public. A good many representatives and senators have been defeated at the polls after voters began to grumble about their having "gone Washington" and "forgotten where they came from." So, not by law maybe, but certainly by almost lethally enforced political necessity, the average member of Congress must maintain two homes, one in Washington and one in the constituency. "The cost of maintaining two places of residence—in Washington and at home—makes membership nearly unique and singularly expensive among upper-middle class jobs," said Nelson Polsby.[41]

Here is another interesting point: a university president or corporate CEO is entitled to a full deduction for income tax purposes for necessary expenses when required to live away from home. Senators and representatives are not. Members of Congress get a $3,000 tax break to offset their Washington living costs, but that figure is still the same as it was when first enacted in 1952. After Congress sought to change the law in 1981 to allow the deduction of actual Washington living expenses, there was such a public hue and cry and hullabaloo against the change—Common Cause, for example, launching a nationwide "Give Taxpayers a Break" campaign—that it was promptly repealed the following year.

It costs a lot to live in Washington. "You can't explain that a two-bedroom row house here costs $150,000, and back home in Mississippi, that gets five bedrooms and five acres," one member of Congress is quoted as saying.[42] A more suitable Virginia suburban home that one senator paid $55,000 for in 1966 was, ten years later, worth three times that amount and, today, would bring over a half million dollars, a tenfold increase in price while a senator's salary was going up at less than half that rate. "Money in Capitol Hill is not being put to evil purposes," a campaign consultant and Washington observer has correctly said. "In most of these cases, it's being put to survive. These members have got families, kids in school."[43]

James K. Glassman of *Roll Call* called attention to the fact that both *Money* magazine—which launched one of the meanest recent attacks on congressional costs—and *Time* magazine—which in 1992 ran trade publication advertisements headlined, "We Smell Blood in Washington," declaring that voters are not just looking for blood, but "want to see heads roll" and that "the best place to follow the show is in these pages"—are both owned by Time-Warner, "a company whose chief executive in 1990 made more money than all 535 members of Congress combined."[44] It is a fact, of course, that the salaries of members of Congress put them in at least the top 2 percent of American earners, and, it is not surprising that, for a lot of Americans much lower on the pay scale, these salaries look excessive. The salaries seem too high, Nelson Polsby says, especially because Congress-bashers often incite "citizens to a mindless social envy, in which it is assumed that paying a decent professional salary to professional officeholders is automatically some sort of rip-off.''[45]

A quite different perspective on the size of congressional salaries—and I note it here, more or less whimsically—is that of millionaire author Tom Clancy, who said about senators and representatives: ''They're failures. Well, that's a little strong. But if $120,000 a year is the best job you've ever had, you haven't really done much.''[46] More seriously, Polsby pointed out that even brand new graduates of good law schools are now offered starting annual salaries of $90,000 or more by New York law firms, and he asked, ''How can we argue that members of Congress and others at the top of the federal government should not be paid at least a modest premium above these beginners' wages?''[47]

Though congressional pay is good and getting better, said congressional experts Edward Schneier and Bertram Gross, it is ''still not comparable to that of a top businessman or professional.''[48] That is correct, and the same point was made by Polsby:

> People with far less serious responsibilities in the private sector are ordinarily paid considerably better than members of Congress. Think, for example, how far down the organizational chart at General Motors or at CBS or at some other large corporation one would have to go before reaching executives making what members of Congress do, and compare their responsibilities with those of Congress and its members. Actually, most corporations won't say what their compensation packages are like. But at a major auto company, people who make $100,000 a year are no higher than upper middle management, and certainly don't have responsibilities remotely comparable to those of members of Congress.[49]

It is also useful to compare congressional salaries with salaries paid in higher education for positions of similar responsibilities. A 1993 survey of 190 colleges and universities by the *Chronicle of Higher Education* found that most of the presidents of those institutions were receiving $155,000 or more a year in pay and benefits, with three research universities paying their presidents more than $400,000 annually and twelve paying more than $300,000. The total group also included thirty-one liberal arts colleges that each paid their presidents salaries of more than $175,000 a year and thirty-two such institutions whose presidents were paid more than $150,000.[50]

Nearly all states have at least two big public universities, just as they have two U.S. Senators. In New Mexico for the 1992–93 school year, the president of the University of New Mexico, Dr. Richard Peck, received an annual salary of $146,000 (later raised to $153,000 for 1993–94), and the president of New Mexico State University, Dr. James Halligan, received $135,370 (plus, in each case, they received retirement and health benefits, of course).[51] In addition, both presidents enjoyed free homes and automobiles and held tenured professorships to fall back on if they stepped down or were fired. In President Peck's case, at least, a maid and a cook, as well as an allowance for entertainment, came with the presidential residence, and his contract provided that, if he remained in his job for five years, he would get an additional amount equal to 12 percent of each year's salary as a bonus for his perseverance.

Needless to say, no residences are provided for senators and representatives. No cars are provided for them either (except for the leaders). Nor do members of Congress have any job security. (Retirement pensions *are* provided for senators and representatives, rather generous ones, too, though they are not out of line with private industry, especially in light of the fact that it is particularly hard for members of Congress to pick up the occupational or professional pieces of their lives again after an absence of years in Washington.)

Incidentally, the athletic director at the University of New Mexico, who is not also a coach, was paid a contract salary of $125,000 in 1993. And it is worth taking note of the salaries of two other positions in New Mexico, one in higher education and one in private industry that were filled with new hires in the same month, July 1993. Dr. Mary Sue Coleman was chosen as the University of New Mexico's new provost and vice-president for academic affairs at an annual salary of $130,000, with tenure as a full professor in her field, and, as a part of the employment package, her husband, a noted Latin Americanist, was hired as a tenured full professor, too, in the university's political science department.[52]

That same month, Public Service Company of New Mexico, the local, privately owned public utility, announced the hiring of a retired admiral, Benjamin F. Montoya, as its new president and CEO, at an annual salary of $320,000. (This salary was $60,000 more than had been paid to the outgoing president. It was less, though, than the salary of the president before that, who, it was announced in 1993, was then receiving $319,000 a year in retirement benefits from the company.)[53]

Compared to salaries paid to national legislators in other countries, to the responsibilities of the job, to members' cost of living, and to the salaries of comparable private and public positions, the pay of U.S. senators and representatives is not exorbitant, but commensurate.

CONGRESSIONAL PERKS AND PATRONAGE

Congress has been harshly criticized for what has been called its "perquisites and patronage."

Patronage

The patronage charge—taking it first—is both silly and outdated. Long, long gone are the days when a representative or senator could appoint people to jobs such as local postmaster or rural mail carrier. On Capitol Hill, nepotism has long since been outlawed. There has been a thirty-year trend away from patronage altogether and toward staff professionalism, according to political scientist Robert Salisbury. "Institutions such as the Congressional Research Service, the Library of Congress and the Congressional Budget Office now all have high-quality professional talent," he said.[54] Even twenty years ago, patronage accounted for only a fourth of those appointed to the Capitol police force. Today, that is down to less than 10 percent, and the political appointees have to comply with the same standards and training as the others.

The fact is, *Congressional Quarterly* pointed out, "political patronage, especially that dispensed by members of Congress, has declined to virtually nothing," and, the publication correctly adds, the loss has not been particularly lamented; many legislators regarded it as a nuisance.[55] The greatly reduced numbers of low-skill patronage jobs still available in the Capitol are so generally unattractive that they are "of little help in strengthening [a member's] political position or rewarding his [or her] campaign supporters back home."[56]

Perhaps it could be said that the personal staffs of senators and representatives constitute part of their patronage. But it is not patronage in the traditional sense. True, a member of Congress has the sole power to name these personal staff people, and they are not protected by civil service laws, serving at the member's pleasure. But that is just as true for a state governor's personal staff, for example, or the president's White House staff and for the same reasons: the political nature of these offices requires the freedom to hire politically loyal aides.

Congress has been criticized for not fully applying to itself all the laws it has imposed on private and executive department employers. It has made itself subject to civil rights, disabilities and rehabilitation, age discrimination, sexual harassment, and family leave laws and has set up a separate House and Senate Fair Employment Practices Office to handle complaints (to avoid violation of the separation of powers principle through executive branch enforcement).[57] The Senate side of the reform panel, the Joint Committee on the Organization of Congress, recommended applying all the pertinent laws to the employees of that body, and doing it more fully.[58] And House Speaker Thomas Foley announced that he backs the plan of the Joint Committee that would establish a new Office of Compliance for Congress, subject Congress to all laws affecting the private sector, and give House employees a right to appeal violations cases to the courts, as Senate employees can already do.[59]

Member Perks

It has been charged that member perquisites, or perks, provide senators and representatives with an insular, cloistered, and pampered existence that separates them from the real world. Nonsense, political scientist Nelson Polsby responded. He knows Congress well, and he wrote:

> I believe we can dismiss out of hand the charge that large numbers of members individually, or Congress collectively, live in a world all their own, divorced from realities of everyday life. The sophomores who have written attacks of this sort in recent years in *Atlantic*, *Newsweek*, and elsewhere simply don't know what they are talking about. They abuse their access to large audiences by neglecting to explain the real conditions that govern the lives of members, conditions that provide ample doses of everyday life.[60]

Similarly, the American Enterprise Institute's resident Congress watcher, Norman Ornstein, said that the recent assault on member perks "has been almost breathtaking in its exaggerations, distortions, hypocrisy, and venom. Some articles cited Congressional perks like stamps and phones—the equivalent of saying that journalists have perks like typewriters and notebooks!"[61]

But what about the freebie life of members, the culture of privilege, as it has been called—their gymnasiums, for example, cheap haircuts and meals, low-cost car washes, free prescription medications, and subsidized life insurance? Such criticisms range from petty nitpicking to shameless exaggeration. And, in any event, the recent "perk panic" in Congress, as one reporter put it, has caused the hammer to come down on most of these so-called perquisites.

Senators and representatives have had their own separate gyms for many years, but it is ridiculous to call them "health spas," as one magazine did. The Senate gym is cramped and dank. In the past, senators could use it free.

The House gym is more spacious and accommodating. Members paid $100 a year to work out there. Now, both the House and Senate have set gym fees at $400 a year. "I think it's appropriate to have a gymnasium," House Speaker Thomas Foley of Washington said in making the announcement on the House side. "Every corporate organization I know of has one. But it is also appropriate that we pay a reasonable charge for it."[62] On the Senate side, the new gym fee did not seem so appropriate to many members and caused Mississippi Republican Senator Trent Lott, for example, to complain, "Four hundred dollars for the Senate gym? That place is an armpit. I caught jungle rot there last year."[63]

Congressional haircuts have now been raised from $5 to $10. Big deal! "The favorite target for journalists has probably been the House barber shop and its $5 (now $10) haircuts, characterized as if the benefit provided were the equivalent of a $60 hair styling at a posh Georgetown salon," wrote Norman Ornstein. "Anyone who has ever had a haircut in the House barber shop knows the appropriate comparison is the corner barber shop or a chain, where assembly-line haircuts are between $7 and $10. For me, the analogy is the Bradley Barber Shop in Bethesda, where Nick does a dynamite job of cutting and styling for nine bucks."[64]

Time magazine's attack on Congress for its "opulent dining rooms with crystal chandeliers and black-tie waiters" prompted this response from Ornstein: "Either the writers have never eaten in the House dining room and tried to digest a Congressional chicken-salad sandwich, or they are deliberately exaggerating in an astonishing fashion."[65] The same could be said about the Senate dining room in the Capitol. Now, a secondary Senate dining room in one of the office buildings has been closed, and in the two remaining dining rooms for senators and representatives, hours have been shortened, and prices have been raised.

And, incidentally, on the subject of restaurants, it is interesting to note the great hullabaloo raised in early 1992 about the House "deadbeats" who had run up unpaid tabs at the House restaurant totaling more than $300,000. It turned out, as a matter of fact, that this amount was actually less than $10,000. The private service company that runs the place apologized publicly and said that the mistake was caused by a glitch in their computerized billing system, that the restaurant operates on a revolving fund, not taxpayer dollars, and that payment and collection procedures had been tightened up.[66]

It is true that senators used to be able to get a car wash for $3 in the parking area beneath either of two of their office buildings. But first one and, now, the other of these car washes has been cut out.[67] Big savings! From now on, too, members will have to pay an annual fee of $520 for the right to treatment and medicines at the Navy's Office of Attending Physicians in the Capitol (formerly used free by some members, primarily on an emergency basis), in addition to the cost of the regular health insurance premiums that they have been paying separately.[68]

A *New York Times* article criticized as a member perk the right of senators and representatives to get what it said was $100,000 in life insurance (actually pegged to salary levels) "with one-third of the premiums paid by taxpayers." Norman Ornstein, again, answered: "The cost of $100,000 in group term insurance for a 50-year-old is about $400, meaning the cost to taxpayers for this particular benefit is a hefty $133. Most similarly situated midlevel corporate executives receive group insurance of between two and five times their salaries and rarely pay for more than half the premiums."[69]

Finally, on perks, mention must be made of the so-called House Bank scandal that broke in late 1991—"Rubbergate," as some called it.[70] Press and public furor over members' "hot," "rubber," "bounced," and "kited" checks at the House bank fueled, more than anything else, the conflagration of disapproval that has engulfed Congress in recent times. Though this affair was "small potatoes by comparison," *Congressional Quarterly* said, it "quickly aroused a louder outcry than the multibillion-dollar bank and savings and loan failures that made headline news throughout 1991."[71]

Stuart Taylor, Jr., wrote in *Legal Times* that the House bank scandal "whipped the radio talk shows into a frenzy, the public into an apoplexy, and the press into a feeding frenzy." Taylor concluded: "And for it to be ballyhooed with such orgasmic glee by *Wall Street Journal* editorialists and other right-wing Congress-bashers [was] a transparent pretext for harping on their constant theme: that the elected representatives of the people are such a mess that the executive branch should be trusted to run things without interference from them."[72]

A number of House members quit or were defeated in the scandal's aftermath. And, even despite the fact that the Senate, itself, was not involved and that it never has had any institution similar to the House bank, the image of the whole Congress suffered. Election day exit polling showed, for example, that the public dissatisfaction with Congress resulting from the bank scandal was a factor in the 1992 primary renomination defeat of Illinois Democratic Senator Alan Dixon by challenger, now Senator, Carol Moseley-Braun.[73]

The first thing to be said about the House bank scandal is that no "bank" was really involved. In the 1790s, House officials began a practice of collecting members' compensation in bulk and then paying it out individually to keep representatives from having to go personally to the Treasury Department for their checks. The system was consolidated under the Office of the House Sergeant at Arms in 1830, and, soon, what was at first merely a disbursing office also began to hold members' money on deposit and cash their checks against it.

Thus, second, it was not the public's money that was involved in this scandal. Under longstanding practice, the monthly salary of a representative could be paid, at the member's option, in one of three ways: by check to the member, by direct deposit to the member's private bank account, or by leaving the money with the House Sergeant at Arms in a member account there. The House bank, as it came to be called, held only the money of House members, not general federal treasury funds or other deposits, and was then, in a sense, a cooperative.

Third, not a dime's worth of anybody's money—not federal money, not members' money—was lost in the whole affair. Most private banks pay interest on deposits and will agree in advance to treat a depositor overdraft like a loan, with an interest charge. The House bank was different. It did not pay interest on member deposits, nor did it charge interest on member overdrafts, treating them as salary advances.

The bank's administration grew sloppy over the years. There were no written rules about overdrafts but an unwritten rule that representatives' checks would always be honored up to the amount of their next month's pay. No routine notices were given to members about their overdrafts. A number of them, it would turn out later, wrote one or more insufficient funds checks during the three and a half years before the scandal broke without ever realizing, or being advised, that they had done so. In any event, all overdrafts honored by the bank were always later covered by the members involved. The bank was never insolvent. No money was lost.

The whole uproar started with a critical October 1991 report about the bank by the auditing and oversight arm of Congress, the General Accounting Office. House Republican Whip Newt Gingrich of Georgia seized upon the issue as another bludgeon to pound the Democratic leadership with. He called for a full-blown investigation and demanded that the names of all those who had ever written an overdraft check at the bank be made public.

What was an initially clumsy response of the House leadership looked like a cover-up. But Speaker Thomas Foley did refer the matter for investigation by the House Ethics Committee, ordering them to name the top two-dozen worst abusers. And, by a December 1991 House vote, the bank was abolished altogether. If the bank had ever constituted an unjustified House perk, it no longer did; the House bank no longer existed.

But congressional critics were already in full cry. "Serious journalists perceived at the outset that this was a tempest in a teapot," Stuart Taylor, Jr., said, "Then the radio talk-show hosts and their ilk showed once again how easy it is to twitch the crazy bone of the electorate. Then the quality press, worried about being out of touch with the real people, dove headlong into the journalistic race to the bottom."[74]

The names of 325 current and former members of Congress were announced as having overdrawn their accounts during the preceding three and a half years. They included twenty-two who were found by the House Ethics Committee to have abused their banking privileges. President Bush's Attorney General named a special prosecutor, despite the fact that the list of present and former members with overdrafts turned out to contain the names of a number of Republicans, including Newt Gingrich himself, as well as three former House members then serving in the President's cabinet.

At last, after a highly damaging fifteen-month public ruckus and uproar and a five-month, finetooth comb investigation by the special prosecutor, this worthy issued his final report in December 1992, stating, "As of the date of this report, the vast majority of [House bank] account holders have received a letter from me advising each of my conclusion that no criminal inquiry is warranted."[75] All but twenty on the list had been so exonerated, and an official familiar with the probe said that at least half of those would also likely receive exoneration letters. These exonerations left less than ten people subject to further criminal investigation, and the special prosecutor stated that this group "consisted almost entirely" of former and departing members. Then nothing further was heard during 1993 and into 1994 about any prosecution of even these few (although in late 1993 the former Sergeant at Arms who had headed the bank pleaded guilty to crimes, unrelated to the scandal, that he, personally, had committed, including fraud and embezzlement[76]).

The bank was dead. The scandal was over. But the image of Congress remained grievously, and unfairly, injured.

CONGRESSIONAL PERSONNEL

Critics say that congressional staff is too large and too costly, that staff numbers are growing inordinately, and that staff members insulate senators and representatives from each other and are policy freelancers, increasing congressional work. These criticisms are unjustified on all counts.

Congress is, indeed, far and away the best staffed national legislature in the world. But it should be that way, because Congress is also the world's most independent and most powerful national legislature. These two facts are interrelated. We must remember that, in our separation of powers system, unlike in a parliamentary system, Congress was intended to be a coequal branch. Congress should not be a dependency of the executive department, a supplicant for information, reliant on the executive branch for legislative and budgetary proposals and initiatives. It once was, though, in large part.

In 1941, after nine years of President Franklin Roosevelt's New Deal expansion of the executive branch, Congress was spending only one cent on itself for every seven dollars it was authorizing the rest of the federal government to spend.[77] The total staff of Congress and the agencies under its jurisdiction amounted to only 3,200, and these staff members were mostly custodial and clerical aides. An increased workload had put a heavy burden on members of Congress and their limited staff. *Congressional Quarterly* reported:

> As communications and transportation improved, voters could demand more from their elected officials. Consequently, casework [on constituents' personal problems] increased. Furthermore, issues and legislation had become more complex. . . .
> Another problem that drove Congress to change its staffing practices was the lack of staff with technical expertise and skills. Congress relied on the executive branch and lobbying groups to provide specialized assistance and help with drafting bills.[78]

Congress grew after the executive branch of the federal government grew, but with a lag. This lag helped to shift the balance of power to the executive. As the imbalance worsened, senators and representatives began to worry about "executive branch dictatorship." They were concerned that Congress was becoming a "second-class institution." Reformer Robert M. La Follette, Jr., Republican senator from Wisconsin, stated the problem this way in 1946:

> Undoubtedly one of the great contributing factors to the shift of influence and power from the legislative to the executive branch in recent years is the fact that Congress has been generous in providing expert and technical personnel for executive agencies but niggardly in providing such personnel for itself.[79]

La Follette, together with A. S. Mike Monroney, then a Democratic House member from Oklahoma, coauthored the Legislative Reorganization

Act of 1946, which, among other things, gave Congress more staff help for dealing with its increased workload and with the growing executive branch. Some members of Congress objected to this staff enlargement on the grounds that it would amount to a public admission that senators and representatives were not personally competent enough to cope with their legislative jobs. The powerful committee chairpersons of the day, who had succeeded to their positions through seniority, were also generally opposed to giving ordinary members more staff, no doubt because they correctly saw that their own authority would be diminished as their near internal monopoly over information and technical assistance was reduced.

But the 1946 staff increase was adopted, and other increases were agreed to in later years. The largest congressional staff growth came following the federal government expansions of the 1960s and 1970s, as noted earlier in the discussion of general congressional costs. The 1970s saw an explosion in the size of the White House and executive office staff, and, in line with what Senator Daniel Patrick Moynihan (D., NY) has called the "Iron Law of Emulation," Congress decided it needed additional bureaucracy of its own to maintain some parity.

The "advocacy explosion"—the enormous growth in the number of Washington lobby groups and the intensity and scope of their activities—was also a cause of congressional staff growth. Former South Dakota Democratic Senator James Abourezk has made this point. He said that "an active, if sometimes redundant, congressional staff is necessary" to offset the powerful "private constituencies that influence Congress."[80]

The workload of members of Congress increased enormously. A management study of Congress in 1984 reported:

· The amount of constituent correspondence entering the House and the Senate skyrocketed over the last few years, from 15 million pieces of mail in 1970 to 300 million pieces today—a 2,000 percent increase!

  Casework requests have doubled over the last decade—some offices report as many as 5,000 to 10,000 requests per year.

  The number of bills introduced in 1956 was 7,611. By 1980, that number had risen to 14,594. While this trend dropped off slightly in the last Congress, members today are expected to know a great deal more about many more issues than their predecessors.

  The number of record votes is up by 1,250 percent since 1956. [Members of Congress] are expected to know the details of these votes and to be able to defend [their] position[s] on them as [the votes] are scrutinized by the press and the public.[81]

David Vogler reported that during the 1989–90 term of Congress, for example, 14,000 bills and resolutions were introduced, and there were 915 recorded votes on the House floor. But he noted that these figures reflect only a small part of the total legislative work of that period: "An average of more than 5,000 committee and subcommittee meetings take place in every Congress. The average House office today receives nearly a million letters and postcards and has more than 5,000 requests for constituency service and casework every year."[82]

The importance of having sufficient staff is also made clear by a look at what Hedrick Smith has said members of Congress now do every day:

> On a normal day, a senator [or representative] has two and sometimes three simultaneous committee hearings, floor votes, issues caucuses, meetings with other congressmen from his state or region, plus lobbyists, constituents, and press to handle. He will dart into one hearing, get a quick fill-in from his staffer, inject his ten minute's worth and rush on to the next event. . . . Only the staff specialist has any continuity with substance. The member is constantly hopscotching.[83]

Today, the average senator has thirty-nine personal staff members; the average House member, sixteen. In addition, congressional committees and subcommittees have professional staff members, and the full House and the full Senate have paid officers, such as the clerk of the House and the secretary of the Senate, as well as leadership staff.

Congress-bashers—this designation includes a number of House and Senate members themselves—frequently inflate staff totals when they make their attacks. Until he was called on it, Senator Hank Brown (R., Colo.), for example, did. What about his own staff? Brown was asked when he appeared on ABC News "Nightline" in 1992. Is it bloated? No, not at all. "Our staff is the standard one of about 35," Brown responded, "but the member's staff is not the huge one. The huge one is the 38,000, 39,000 staff members, many of them appointed, patronage, rather than civil service, and the real abuse here is not the ones that answer the mail."[84]

The congressional staff includes 38,000 or 39,000? The latest figures available, published in *Vital Statistics on Congress 1993–1994*,[85] show that the people who serve on the personal staffs of senators and representatives total about 7,300 in the House, 4,300 in the Senate—11,600 all together. To that, add the committee and subcommittee staffs, numbering about 2,300 people in the House, 1,100 in the Senate, as well as the officers and leadership staffs of each of the chambers—totaling about 1,450 in the House and 1,100 in the Senate. All these add up to 17,550 staff members. Add in the staffs of joint committees (about 150); the staffs of the Congressional Budget Office (226) and the Office of Technology Assessment (150); the part of the Library of Congress that works directly for Congress, the Congressional Research Service (830); and the 30 percent of the employees of the General Accounting Office who work directly for Congress (1,600)—the grand total only comes to 20,500. Add in the janitors, repair people, painters, and others who work for the Architect of the Capitol (2,099), responsible for the upkeep and maintenance of the great old historic building in which Congress meets, and all the employees of the Capitol Police Force (1,265), responsible for security in and around this public edifice, and the overall total still stands at only 23,870.

Even with *all* the employees of the Library of Congress and the General Accounting Office added in, the grand total still just comes to around 32,000. To get to the 38,000 or 39,000 figure that critics such as Senator Hank Brown bandy about, they must also add in all the employees of the Government Printing Office, the Copyright Royalty Tribunal, and the Botanic Garden.

Real congressional staff, then, even including the Capitol Police and the office of the architect of the Capitol, totals only around 24,000. "By contrast," James Glassman of *Roll Call* pointed out, "the Agriculture Department has 120,000; the Tennessee Valley Authority, 26,000; the Department of Veterans Affairs, 243,000; the U.S. Postal Service, 823,000. The Office of Personnel Management has more employees than the United States Senate."[86]

So, why pick on Congress? "This is really a political move," Glassman asserted. "I think it's led by a lot of people, a lot of conservatives, who want to cut Congress down to size in order to build up the power of the executive. That's where this whole thing began."[87]

Congress does not have a bloated staff, given the responsibilities of Congress and the size of the executive branch that it must oversee. Nor is congressional staff continuing to swell. The 1988 special report of the House Democratic Study Group made this clear. It stated:

Over the past ten years, the total number of legislative branch employees has actually *dropped* by 3%. At the same time, employment in the Executive Branch increased 9% while employment in the Judicial Branch rose 61%.

In 1977, there were 73 Executive Branch employees (excluding the military) for every employee of the Legislative Branch; in 1987, there were 82 Executive Branch employees for every Legislative Branch staffer.[88]

Similarly, in 1991, the grand total of all personal, committee, leadership, and officer staff in the Senate was less than six hundred more than it had been a decade earlier, and the same total for the House was only a little over one hundred fifty more than it had been ten years before.[89] Furthermore, in 1993, pressured by public criticism and by President Clinton's decreed reduction in White House staff numbers, Congress approved a 14 percent cut in administrative expenses over four years and a 4 percent staff cut over two years.[90]

Although recommending some staff reductions in that range, a 1992 report of the "Renewing Congress Project" of the American Enterprise Institute and the Brookings Institution warned against much greater staff reductions, as follows:

> Major cuts in committee staffs would almost certainly make Congress more dependent on the executive branch and on interest groups for information and guidance. There would be a reconcentration of staffs and power at the full committee level, increasing the power of the committee chairmen, while also limiting the professional staff available at the subcommittee level to the subcommittee chairmen.[91]

What do congressional staff people do? David Vogler answered the question in this way:

> Members' personal staff and committee staff both spend a lot of their time on policymaking activities. They research issues and generate information relevant to administrative oversight; draft bills; prepare speeches, statements, and reports; organize and help to run committee hearings; communicate with interest groups, executive agencies, and other legislative staffs; and sometimes engage directly in legislative bargaining. In addition to these legislative activities, personal staff also help members meet their responsibilities by handling the mail and constituent casework for the office.[92]

Do staff members do *too* much? Are they too powerful? Are there hordes of these "unelected representatives" out on frolics of their own, operating as "policy entrepreneurs," independently dreaming up all sorts of unnecessary new work for senators and representatives to do and uncalled-for new legislation for them to introduce? Some people, even senators, say so.[93] Do not believe it.

Certainly, there is no near permanent cadre of congressional staffers. Turnover among them is quite high. The Obey Commission in the House, for example, found that more than 40 percent of staff members were in their twenties and that half the members of committee staffs and 60 percent of the members of personal staffs had been in their jobs for less than two years.[94] There is also high turnover on Senate staffs.[95]

When examined, the charge about staff members being "unelected representatives" usually deals only with Senate, not House, staff. It is natural, though, that senators should rely more on their staff than House members do, both because there are fewer senators to cover all the issues and because Senate rules encourage more individual involvement in policy-making. Ross Baker wrote about this difference as follows:

> Spread so thinly across a range of committees whose subject matters may differ widely, the senator's relationship to staff is far different from that of the more focused House member. Because their ability to develop specialized knowledge is limited by the time they can devote to any one committee responsibility, senators must rely on staff to fill the gaps.
>
> But senators can also tackle a wider range of national issues; they gain broader exposure through their multiple committee assignments and are generally less constrained than House members on the topics on which they can speak. Liberal rules of debate permit them to use the floor as a forum to raise new issues that need not even be related to pending legislation. Staff provides them with many of these issues.[96]

Are Senate staff members an unwarranted barrier between senators? Democratic Senator David Boren of Oklahoma seems to think so. "When you talk to a colleague about an amendment," he said, "the answer is 'Who's your guy on that? Have them call my guy.' "[97] Negotiations between a senator, on the one hand, and the White House or an executive branch agency, a lobby group, or even another senator, on the other hand, often begin for both sides at the staff level. Ross Baker has called this "senatorial summitry."[98] After the details have been worked out by the staffs, the principals come together for the handshake, in a sense, to seal the deal. What's wrong with that? Without specialized and trusted staff members, senators would be at the mercy of executive branch personnel, lobbyists, or other senators for information and advice.

But staff members do not act on their own. The "impact of staff is overrated," their power and influence "an illusion," according to former Senate Republican Leader Howard Baker of Tennessee.[99] One study has shown that subcommittee staff are generally "human extensions of their bosses" and promote policy positions "at the behest of the chair."[100] Ross Baker added that "the ultimate source of authority is the senator. The fact that most office-to-office contact on the Senate side is at the staff level should not obscure the fact that on important issues there is consultation between the principals. On nonroutine matters, the ground rules are established by the senators."[101]

Democratic Senator Ernest Hollings of South Carolina has grouched that some senators "feel that all they are doing is running around and responding to the staff," that more staff means more work.[102] It is hard to take such a complaint seriously. If senators really believed that they were dominated by their staffs or that having too many staff members created unnecessary, uncalled-for work, they could simply ask that the money allowed them for personal staff be reduced or, more simply, decline to hire so many people.

So far as is known, no senator—or representative—has ever done that. In fact, senators generally want more personal staff to cope with their increased workloads.[103] And when senators recommended staff cuts to their reform panel, the Joint Committee on the Organization of Congress, with few exceptions senators said that they meant that the reductions should come in the staffs of committees and congressional support agencies, such as the Government Printing Office and the Architect of the Capitol.[104]

CONCLUSION

Congress-bashing has become a pretty rough parlor game. Most of it has been unjustified and unfair. The remedies advocated often go far beyond reforming the specific problems complained of. The general unpopularity of Congress, questions about member ethics, and rising public concern about the tremendous advantage that incumbent House members, particularly, enjoy when they seek reelection have swollen support in recent times for congressional term limits, an unjustified and unneeded "reform."

Senators and representatives should, of course, be held to high standards of ethics and should be kept fully accountable to the people through regular elections that pose potentially real challenges. There are better ways than term limits to ensure this.

CHAPTER 2

Toward More Accountable Members

James Madison wrote in *Federalist 57* that the aim of a country's constitution should be, first, "to obtain for rulers, men who possess most wisdom to discern, and most virtue to pursue the common good of society" and, then, "to take the most effectual precautions for keeping them virtuous." Madison believed that the best precaution for keeping members of the House of Representatives virtuous was to require all of them to stand for election every two years. Election, he wrote, is "the characteristic policy of republican government."

Members of the Senate were also meant to be accountable to the people, of course, though initially only indirectly; senators were at first chosen by state legislatures. But the Seventeenth Amendment, adopted in 1913, provided that senators, too, should be elected directly (though still only a third of them each two years and all for six-year terms).

Two presumptions underlie such a system of holding senators and representatives accountable through periodic elections: first, the presumption that the voters will be able to get the information they need to judge the performance and virtues of incumbent members of Congress, and second, the presumption that sitting senators and representatives will be electorally challengeable, that there will, in other words, be a real potential for competitive elections. Until the congressional reforms of the 1970s, the first presumption about voter access to information remained far from realization. Congress was a very closed institution. First, unrecorded voice votes and teller votes were commonplace in the House of Representatives. Unless citizens happened to be in the House gallery when such a vote was taken, they usually had no way of knowing how a particular representative voted.

Second, prior to the 1970s reforms, mark-up sessions in congressional committees and subcommittees—where the crucial final decisions are taken on amendments to pending legislation and on whether to report the legislation to the full House or Senate—were closed as a matter of course. Thus what individual senators and representatives did in their committees, how they voted, went largely unreported and unnoticed. Further, television cameras were not allowed into even the *public* hearings of House committees, nor were they allowed to cover the full sessions of either chamber.

All that changed, as Congress began to apply sunshine laws to itself. House rules were amended to require recorded votes, and a system of public, electronic voting was also adopted in that body. Committee and subcommittee mark-up sessions in both houses were opened up to the public as a matter of routine, and radio and television were allowed to cover such sessions, the same as the writing press could. The Senate and House began to televise their plenary sessions, too.

Congress became much more open to the public and the press, then, just at a time, incidentally, when the public was becoming more attentive to congressional operations. Simultaneously, there were two significant developments in the press: an enormous growth in the number of reporters covering Congress and the assumption by reporters of a much more aggressive role.

In the sixteen years between 1960 and 1976, for example, the number of radio and television journalists reporting on Congress tripled, and the number of print journalists increased by a third.[1] This kind of growth continued so that by the mid-1980s, around ten thousand reporters were working in Washington.

Nationally, both the number and length of television network news programs expanded. Cable news networks were launched. Continuous, twenty-four-hour-a-day radio and television news programs appeared. Two new national cable channels began to cover Congress live. Local newspapers and television stations opened their own Washington bureaus or hired stringers for regular capital reports.

The number of spotlights on Congress multiplied and so did their intensity. "In the old days," former Senate parliamentarian Floyd Riddick said, "no reporter would dare stop a senator on his way to or from the Senate and ask for a comment. The Senator would have said, 'See me in my office.' Senators are now more accessible."[2] Representatives are, too. And nothing—neither public decision making nor personal peccadillos—is off limits for today's reporters.

It is much more likely, these days, that U.S. voters will get the information they need to judge senators and representatives at election time. But, if the voters are dissatisfied because of what they know, can they really do anything about it? Critics say that the answer is often no, that frequently no real electoral challenge or competition exists, because the incumbent has too great an advantage.

Abuse of the franking privilege and the use of staff for campaign purposes are listed as two "grossly unfair" advantages enjoyed by congressional incumbents.[3] After reporting on a 1992 ABC News "Nightline" show that a former congressional aide "says almost all congresspeople and senators regularly abuse the franking privilege, just as he says almost all of them use their professional staffers to campaign," television journalist Dave Marash concluded on his own that Congress thereby "buys itself a better chance to get reelected" and that, thus, "the biggest cost of keeping Congress may not be to taxpayers, but to democracy."[4]

House and Senate campaigns cost tremendous amounts of money today, and incumbents have a much better chance of raising it than potential challengers do. This advantage is seen by congressional critics not only as an enormous one for the incumbent, making real electoral competition more unlikely, but also as a source of potential corruption of senators and representatives, making them too beholden to the special interests. And critics also charge that the ethics of many members of Congress are somewhere between questionable and rotten.

A burgeoning and increasingly vociferous group of anti-Congress activists say that a quick cure-all that they advocate would deal with all these problems at once: the imposition of limits on how long each senator and representative can serve in Congress.

TERM LIMITS

The term limit movement has a decidedly conservative and Republican cast, and it springs from a kind of throw-the-rascals-out disapproval of Congress *as a whole*, as an institution.[5] Never mind that nothing about term limits would prevent the voters from electing new senators and representatives just as "bad" as those that limited terms would discard. Never mind, either, as James Sundquist said, that the voters of each district and state can already reject their *own* members of Congress:

> Each voter can act to throw out one rascal, but the others are beyond reach. And it is the others who have aroused the citizens; the single one on whom the individual voter is permitted to pass judgment is, in all likelihood, one with whom he or she usually agrees and who is often, too, a friend, neighbor, or at least a casual acquaintance to

whom the citizen has access when it may be needed, and one who may have brought tangible benefits to the state or district—and, with reelection and greater seniority, will be able to bring more.[6]

Antagonism in Colorado toward Congress as a whole caused that state to be the first, in 1990, to adopt term limits for its own U.S. senators and representatives. The voters in fourteen other states adopted similar congressional term limits two years later, in the elections of November 1992. Despite such growing support, the idea of term limits is still one whose time has not yet—and should never—come. In the first place, it is unconstitutional.

The Founders' Decision against Term Limits

Legislative term limits, or "rotation" in office, as it was then called, was neither a new nor acceptable concept for the Founders when they met in Philadelphia in 1787. Thirty-two of the thirty-nine eventual signers of the Constitution had earlier been delegates at one time or another to the old Continental Congress, in which, under the Articles of Confederation, service had been limited to "three years in any term of six years." The Founders knew that the old Congress had gotten itself into such a bitter internal fight in 1784 over the question of enforcing these term limits against sitting members that the whole matter had had to be dropped.[7]

The Founders decided against term limits for federal officials, and later argued against them in the ratification fight, on three grounds. First, they did so because term limits would be an unreasonable restriction on the power of the people—would unacceptably "abridge the privilege of the people," as Roger Sherman put it.[8] Robert R. Livingston made the same argument when he wrote: "The people are the best judges of who ought to represent them. To dictate and control them, to tell them whom they shall not elect, is to abridge their natural rights."[9]

Second, the Founders argued that term limits for federal officials, by limiting reelection possibilities, would reduce incentive for good conduct in office. Limiting terms "would be a diminution of the inducements to good behavior," according to Alexander Hamilton,[10] would "remove one great motive to fidelity in office," as Roger Sherman put it.[11] Robert R. Livingston stated the argument even more strongly: "This rotation is an absurd species of ostracism—a mode of proscribing eminent merit, and banishing from stations of trust those who have filled them with the greatest faithfulness. Besides it takes away the strongest stimulus to public virtue—the hopes of honors and rewards."[12]

The third argument of the Founders against term limits was that they would deny people the right to retain experienced public officials, as Livingston had said, and would "render persons incapable of serving in offices, on account of their experience, which would best qualify them for usefulness in office," as Roger Sherman wrote.[13]

Can States Adopt Term Limits?

Since the writers of the Constitution, then, unlike those who drafted the earlier Articles of Confederation, rejected term limits, can states, by amendments to their own constitutions, now adopt limits on how long their members of Congress can serve? The U.S. Supreme Court has never squarely decided this question, but it is fairly clear that the answer should be no. The Court may soon have to face the issue. The League of Women Voters, joined by Democratic U.S. House Speaker Thomas Foley of Washington, has filed a lawsuit in federal court to nullify the 1992 initiative adopted in Foley's home state that would limit the terms of that state's members of Congress.[14]

The U.S. Constitution, in Article I, Sections 2 and 3, is quite specific about the requisite qualifications for serving in the U.S. House and Senate, in each case prescribing only requirements of age, citizenship, and residence. Senators and representatives must be "inhabitants" of the states from which they are elected. A representative must be at least twenty-five years of age and must have been a U.S. citizen for at least seven years. A senator must be at least thirty years old and at least nine years a citizen. Section 4 of the same article gives the state legislatures the power to decide only on the "times, places, and manner of holding elections" for senators and representatives (subject to change in such regulations by Congress). Section 5 makes each house of Congress the sole judge of the "elections, returns, and qualifications" of its own members.

Can a state require a certain number of voter signatures on a petition for a person to become a candidate for the House or Senate, regulate political party nominations generally, and prohibit, say, a person from running as an independent candidate who has been affiliated with a political party within the preceding year? Certainly, it can. Such state laws are "an essential part of its overall mechanism" of traditional election regulation, and, as such, are permissible under the U.S. Constitution.[15]

But suppose the declaration of candidacy form for the U.S. House of Representatives from Washington state, for example, were to call not only for affirmations that the prospective candidate meets the constitutional age, citizenship, and residency qualifications for the office, but also were to require a fourth affirmation, such as, "I certify that I have not previously served twelve or more years as a member of the U.S. House of Representatives"?

That new requirement would obviously amount to more than mere state "regulation" of elections. It would constitute an additional qualification for the office, and a state has no power to add new qualifications for membership in the U.S. House and Senate to those already set forth in the U.S. Constitution. Constitutional experts such as Duke University law professor Walter Dellinger hold this view.[16]

In the 1969 case of *Powell v. McCormack*,[17] the U.S. Supreme Court recounted how those who wrote the U.S. Constitution considered, and rejected, any qualifications for the U.S. Senate and House of Representatives other than those related to age, citizenship, and residence. The Court then held in that case that an attempt by the House of Representatives, itself, to tack on an additional qualification for membership in that body was unconstitutional.

The same should also be true for states. An early decision by the U.S. House of Representatives, at a time when its members were still contemporaries of the writers of the Constitution, gives us some further insight into the Founders' intent on this matter. The decision grew out of a 1790 Maryland statute that required a year's prior residence for U.S. House candidates from that state. One William McCreery had been elected without meeting this Maryland requirement. His election was challenged in the House of Representatives, where he was eventually seated by a vote of 89 to 18. A part of the report of the House Committee of Elections on that occasion stated:

> The committee proceeded to examine the Constitution, with relation to the case submitted to them, and find that qualifications of members are therein determined, without reserving any authority to the State Legislatures to change, add to, or diminish those qualifications; and that, by that instrument, Congress is constituted the sole judge of the qualifications prescribed by it, and are obliged to decide agreeably to the Constitutional rules.[18]

In his remarks on the House floor, the committee chair in the McCreery matter amplified:

> The Committee of Elections considered the qualifications of members to have been unalterably determined by the Federal Convention, unless changed by an authority equal to that which framed the

Constitution at first; that neither the State nor the Federal Legislatures are vested with authority to add to those qualifications so as to change them.[19]

After all, senators and representatives hold federal offices, not state offices, and, as the eminent Justice Joseph Story wrote in his early, landmark constitutional treatise: "The states have just as much right, and no more, to prescribe new qualifications for a representative, as they have for a president. Each is an officer of the Union, deriving his powers and qualifications from the Constitution, and neither created by, dependent upon, nor controllable by, the states."[20]

Theoretically, the U.S. Constitution could be amended to limit congressional terms, but, in reality, there is virtually no chance that proponents of such an amendment could put together the two-thirds majority necessary in both houses of Congress to refer it to the people for vote. Congress cannot pass a simple law to limit the terms of senators and representatives. That would surely be unconstitutional. So, too, the Supreme Court is highly likely to rule in the near future, would be state attempts to do so.[21] Constitutional or not, though, term limits are neither necessary nor wise.

Current Turnover in Congress

Both because of incumbent defeats in recent times (forty-three members of Congress defeated in the big year of 1992, for example) and voluntary retirements (sixty-six in 1992), a large turnover in Congress already occurs. Senior members of Congress have been more likely to go down to defeat in recent elections than first termers.[22] Again, in the 1992 congressional elections, representatives who were defeated in the general election averaged nearly ten and a half years of House service; those who lost in the primaries, fourteen.[23] These primary-defeat numbers prompted one congressional observer to write: "The prototypical incumbent who has lost a House primary this year is not a relatively inexperienced first- or second-termer who has trouble raising money. He is, on average, a 58-year-old Hill veteran with 14 years' seniority and a substantial financial advantage over his primary opposition."[24]

The median number of terms in office for members of the U.S. House of Representatives has fluctuated between four and five since 1953. In 1991, the median was five terms, the same as it was in 1957, 1961, 1963, 1969, 1971, 1973, 1987, and 1989. In the other years since 1957, including 1993, the median was four.[25] "The image of a House top-heavy with long-term incumbents is false,'' Representative Pat Schroeder (D., Colo.) pointed out in 1990. ''Since 1980, more than half of the House has turned over due to defeat, resignation, retirement or death. The average length of service is 5.8 terms.''[26]

Similarly, political scientist Marjorie Randon Hershey wrote:

> It is ironic that . . . the average member of the House now serves no longer than he or she would be allowed to serve by many term-limitation measures: six two-year terms. And largely because of retirements, between 10 and 20 percent of House members in any given Congress are serving their first term—a larger proportion than one might expect after listening to arguments for limits. It seems clear, then, that term limits are no more—and no less—than a symbolic expression of public frustration.[27]

Along the same line, after noting that a twelve-year limit on House service would produce at least 100 percent turnover every twelve years, a little over 16 percent every two years, political scientist John Hibbing observed: ''Such a limit would constitute a small increase over turnover rates in the 1980s but would be about equal to turnover rates in the 1970s—and possibly less than those of the 1990s, if 1992 is any indication. . . . So term limits would stimulate less additional turnover than most people realize.''[28]

The question, then, as James L. Sundquist put it, is ''whether senators and representatives who are competent, energetic, and representative should be cast out of Congress along with their colleagues who may lack those qualities, simply on the ground of length of service.''[29] Term limiters, in effect, say yes. They want to substitute new, younger members for old ones, regardless of merit. Their hope is that doing so would change the internal workings of Congress, too. Less of a case can be made for this argument today than formerly, according to Sundquist, again:

> Were this being written thirty years ago, one could easily come down on the side of youth, for the critical repositories of legislative power in the two houses—specifically, committee chairmanships—were then bestowed automatically on the basis of seniority, and members who were ideologically rigid, unrepresentative of their bodies' membership, worn out, or even senile could gain and retain immense power. But since then the Congress has reformed itself. First, committee chairs have been stripped of much of their arbitrary authority and subjected to democratic control, both by the committee

members acting collectively and by the majority party caucuses and the leaders and leadership bodies elected by them. Second, the automatic seniority system has been jettisoned; although seniority is still the principal criterion in choosing committee chairs, enough senior chairmen have been rejected by their party caucuses to make clear that competence, energy, and a reasonable degree of representativeness are requisites for leadership position.[30]

Sundquist specifically noted that the requirement of competence was reaffirmed in 1992, when the threat of removal caused Democratic Representative Jamie Whitten of Mississippi, who had suffered a stroke, to give up the chair of the House Appropriations Committee. What Sundquist wrote generally about committee chairs being deposed actually applies only to House chairs, but in the Senate, too, the power and formerly autocratic behavior of committee chairs have been seriously curtailed by, among other changes, the establishment of permanent subcommittees for all the standing committees and by rules changes that facilitate caucus votes on the retention of committee chairs in their positions.

Term Limits and Accountability

Limiting congressional terms would be bad policy. The Founders were right when they decided that term limits would unreasonably restrict the power of the people to elect whomever they might choose to public office, would deny the people the opportunity to retain in elective posts those most experienced and expert, and would limit an important incentive for good conduct by incumbent public officials, the desire for reelection.

On this latter point, proponents of term limits frequently bog into logical quicksand. As R. Douglas Arnold wrote:

Many proponents of term limits for legislators have fallen into this trap, arguing that legislators operate beyond the control of constituents—the evidence being that so few legislators are ever defeated at the polls. The problem with this argument is that the contrary hypothesis is observationally equivalent. A setting in which legislators responded perfectly to constituency opinion would produce no defeats at the polls just as certainly as one in which legislators operated independently of constituency opinion.[31]

We need term limits, proponents argue, because senators and representatives do not concern themselves enough with the public interest, since they are too worried about running for reelection. We need term limits, proponents also argue, because incumbent members are not sufficiently accountable to the people, since they are so secure in their jobs and enjoy such advantages of incumbency, that they are invulnerable to defeat and know it.

Which is it? Are incumbent senators and representatives too *little* worried about being reelected, or are they too *much* worried about being reelected? If they are too little worried about reelection, it is hard to see how limiting their opportunity for reelection through term limits is the proper remedy. If incumbents are too much worried about reelection, can that desire be curbed through term limits? Should it be?

Take the first question first: even if controls ought to be placed on the electoral ambitions of senators and representatives, is that possible? The fact is that if too great a concern with reelection is an incumbent sickness that term limits are meant to heal, it is likely that the remedy will produce an equally objectionable side effect: too much concern with running for some *other* elective post. In other words, term limits might replace "reelection behavior with pre-election behavior," as a couple of experts have phrased it well.[32] Most people who run for high public office—such as that of governor or U.S. senator or representative—are people who have decided on elective public service as a career. Is it not unreasonable to suppose that their political ambitions would abruptly wither and die, simultaneously with the expiration of their limited congressional terms?

A reverse case demonstrates the point. Back in the 1950s and earlier, former governors nearly always accounted for close to a fourth of the membership of the Senate, but not any more. Nowadays, usually no more than a tenth of the 100 senators have previously been governors. What changed? State constitutions did. They were amended to allow state chief executives to succeed themselves, and more of these governors thereafter began to run for reelection, rather than for the Senate.[33] Put a limit on Senate terms, and, just as certainly, a certain number of additional senators, most of whom would not now quit to be governor back home, will in their last years as senators begin to focus their election sights on state capitals. The electoral ambitions of a good many senators will not automatically be snuffed out by term limits.

The same would also clearly apply to many more incumbent U.S. representatives. At any one time, now, about a third of the Senate is usually made up of former House members,[34] even though, with two-year terms, these individuals had to give up their House seats to run for the Senate. No one doubts that more House members would launch campaigns for the Senate were this unnecessary. Cap their House careers, and representatives will have nothing to lose by concentrating during their last, limited terms on getting elected to the Senate and, in the process, incidentally, on making themselves more attractive to state-wide, rather than district-wide, electorates.

Now, for the other question: *should* the electoral ambitions of members of Congress be curtailed by term limits? The Founders rightly thought that no such curtailment should be attempted. Those who wrote our Constitution were convinced that the desire for reelection would operate as a salutary restraint on officeholders. The removal of that incentive for conscientious service—through term limits—would encourage officeholders to "sordid views" and "peculation," said Alexander Hamilton, to "make hay while the sun shines," declared Governeur Morris.[35]

A popular Mexican couplet is instructive in this respect. The Constitution of Mexico incorporates a major theme of the 1910 Mexican Revolution— *"¡No Reelección!"* It limits that country's president to one six-year term, or *sexenio* (as some have unwisely advocated should be done here in the United States). Today in Mexico, many laughingly call the last year of a president's term "the year of the hidalgo," in an apparent allusion to the often-corrupt noblemen sent by Spain to govern Mexico during colonial times. Referring to the supposed thinking of the president and his team in the final year of a *sexenio*, cynical Mexicans recite a rhyming couplet that says:

Éste es el año del hidalgo;
Bueyes los que no roban algo.

This is the year of the hidalgo;
Dumb oxen, those who don't rob something.

Would it really be advisable to make members of Congress less answerable to the people by imposing an unbreachable ceiling on their prospects for reelection? Perhaps, as proponents hope, incumbents so limited would turn their attention more assiduously to the public's business; but is it not just as logical to assume the opposite? Might some not, freed from the restraint of having to face reelection, turn their attention more enterprisingly to their own personal interests—for example, to making money, in a few cases, or, in others, to spending their final terms ingratiating themselves with corporations or special interest groups or the law firms and lobbyists of either so as to lock up good private jobs to replace the ones the incumbents would soon be forced to vacate?

Political scientist Linda Fowler has called attention to the fact that a good many members of Congress stay on in Washington after leaving office, using their knowledge of the system and their contacts to make money. She thinks that this "de-recruitment," as she calls it, by the special interests, heightened by term limits, "could mean even more, rather than less, influence peddling" in Washington.[36] Political scientist Nelson Polsby touched somewhat on this same point in this way:

> It is a delusion to think that good public servants are a dime a dozen in each congressional district, and that only the good ones would queue up to take their twelve-year fling at congressional office. But suppose they did. In case they acquired expertise, what would they do next? Make money, I suppose. Just about the time that their constituents and the American people at large could begin to expect a payoff because of the knowledge and experience that these able members had acquired at our expense, off they would go to some Washington law firm.[37]

Inexperienced Legislators and Special Interest Influence

We neither can nor should set rigid time boundaries on the electoral ambitions of members of Congress. But perhaps an even greater concern about congressional term limits, from a good government standpoint, is one expressed by two congressional experts, Edward Schneier and Bertram Gross, having to do with the balance of power in Washington. "To lose the knowledge that comes with legislative experience is to relinquish influence to those who have subject-matter expertise, especially lobbyists and civil servants," they wrote. "Term limitation proposals should probably be called bureaucratic empowerment acts."[38] What about the usefulness, then, of senators and representatives with limited terms? asked Nelson Polsby—and then he answered his own question in this way:

> It would be limited, I'm afraid, by the greater expertise and better command of the territory by lobbyists, congressional staff, and downtown bureaucrats—career people one and all. So this is, once again, a proposal merely to weaken the fabric of Congress in the

political system at large, and thereby to limit the effectiveness of the one set of actors most accessible to the citizens.[39]

It stands to reason that the Speaker of the House in Oklahoma was right when he said that "entrenched interests" will gain from new term limits for state legislators in that state:

> Entrenched interests such as the bureaucracy may gain. They'll always be there. . . . Interest groups, special interests, organized interests are a steady source of influence and that influence will increase. They will be there and the legislature will not. Those who stay around will have more influence than those who are new to the scene.[40]

In the halls of Congress, too, the lobbyists would still be on the scene, if term-limited senators and representatives were forced out, and, as always, the lobbyists would be only too happy to help "educate" the new members who replace those leaving. In Oklahoma, state capital lobbyists think their jobs are going to be harder as a result of legislative term limits because they will have to "spend all of [their] time educating people just to bring them up to speed." This difficulty will be offset, though, one said, by greater effectiveness: "It's easier to influence a freshman. They won't know the ropes. I'll be able to say I was there."[41]

The same effect would apply in a Washington, D.C., with term limits. The headline of a front page *New York Times* article during the 1993 fight on President Clinton's budget announced that a strategy of its lobbyist opponents was to "Go After the Greenhorns," an internal subhead reporting: "The theory: it's easier to win over inexperienced legislators." It was stated in the body of the article that lobbyists "are hoping that the relative inexperience of the new members will leave them open to special entreaties," and the head of one lobbying group was quoted as saying, "The new members tend to be more responsive to our efforts."[42]

With term limits, there would presumably be more such inexperienced and lobbyist-vulnerable new senators and representatives. Reduce the expertise and experience of members of Congress, and you will enhance the influence of the special interests. That seems obvious. It is equally obvious that the balance of governmental power in Washington would undoubtedly be tipped away from Congress toward the bureaucracy.

Conclusion

Term limit advocates are like the old country doctor who threw all his patients into convulsions, no matter what their initial complaints, because he thought he knew how to cure convulsions. Term limits are the wrong medicine, and the remedy would be worse than the presumed malady. But without term limits, critics ask, what can be done about what are said to be the abysmal ethical standards of senators and representatives?

MEMBER ETHICS

People still snicker when someone quotes Mark Twain's famous statement that Congress is our only "distinctly native American criminal class." And if you tell them that the ethics of members of Congress have never been higher, you are likely to get a rejoinder like, "Well, we're sure in a hell of a fix, then!" But it is the truth.

The ethics of members of Congress *are* generally high, higher than ever. Suzanne Garment, who has studied and written about government scandals, has said that "on the whole, the federal government in recent years has been at least as clean as in the past and probably a good deal cleaner."[43] The ethics of most senators are probably better than those of most citizens, said Dennis Thompson, who specializes in governmental ethics at Harvard University.[44]

How could that be true—given all the news about the recent Packwood sexual misconduct case, for example, the allegations about the Rostenkowski misuse of House post office funds and other transgressions, or the "Keating Five" influence-peddling hearings of a couple of years ago? The answer, in a way, is found in an old story about a Roosevelt administration health official, who, after initiating a testing program that showed an alarming incidence of tuberculosis among the poor, attended a backwoods public meeting where a complainant said to him, "And I'll tell you another thing, sir: we never use to have so much TB around here until you New Dealers took over!"

Today, the ethical standards required of members of Congress are much clearer, and higher, than they once were. That is the view of Suzanne Garment, who wrote, "A good deal of our current scandal . . . stems from heightened ethical sensibilities and a distaste for what were once accepted practices in American politics."[45] Furthermore, the public now learns more than it used to about the ethical lapses of members of Congress.

Changes in Congress

The times have changed. The Senate and House themselves have long since established their own committees for dealing publicly with ethics complaints. Thirty years ago, by contrast, when a scandal erupted in the Senate about Robert G. "Bobby" Baker, a Senate aide, using his office to further his own business interests, neither house of Congress had such a committee. Nor did they have defined codes of conduct for members or rules requiring disclosure by members of their financial interests.

In fact, in the Baker hearings, which were conducted by the Senate Committee on Rules and Administration, when an allusion was made to a shady deal involving a senator, the chair of the committee, Democrat Everett Jordan of North Carolina, cut off the discussion by saying, "We're not investigating senators."[46] Now, investigation of senators *is* done by the Senate Committee on Ethics, established in 1964 (then called the Senate Committee on Standards and Conduct). The House, also, now has its own ethics committee, the House Committee on Standards of Official Conduct, established soon after its Senate counterpart. The ethics committees receive complaints, conduct hearings, and have the power to recommend expulsion, censure, or reprimand.

Twenty-five years ago, muckraking columnists Drew Pearson and Jack Anderson wrote a highly critical book, *The Case Against Congress*, in which they detailed many instances of glaringly unethical congressional conduct and then made recommendations for needed changes. Pearson and Anderson recommended, for example, that senators and representatives file and publish the names of all relatives on their payrolls.[47] Today, of course, nepotism is against the law. Pearson and Anderson urged that senators and representatives be required to make financial disclosures. Now, they are. Members must file annual financial statements, showing earned and other income, gifts, financial holdings, liabilities, real estate owned, and securities and commodities transactions.

In their 1968 book, Pearson and Anderson also recommended that members of Congress be prohibited from practicing law before any federal court or agency. Today, *all* law practice by members is prohibited. Not only that, but both houses now prohibit members from keeping any outside, earned income, including honoraria for speeches and appearances. Senators and representatives are banned from lobbying the legislative branch for at least a year after leaving it.

Today, each house has its own code of conduct, and its ethics committees give members advisory opinions in advance about what is, or is not, acceptable practice or conduct. The House has an ethics manual for its members that is easy to follow; the Senate ought to match it and produce ethics rules that are, as Democratic Senator Howell Heflin of Alabama said, "more specific and codified."[48] The Senate in 1992 set up a procedure for handling complaints about sexual misconduct; Democratic Senator Patty Murray of Washington has offered to help improve this procedure, and her offer should be accepted. And each house should institute a regular ethics briefing for its new members at the beginning of each new Congress.

It has been suggested by both the Senate and House sides of the Joint Committee on the Organization of Congress that, in order to eliminate the appearance of favoritism when hearing an ethics complaint against a member, each of the two House and Senate ethics committees should be supplemented by a panel of outsiders that would investigate ethics charges against members. This is a good idea. Still, though, Article I, Section 5, of the Constitution makes each house the sole judge of its own members, as noted, and the House and Senate cannot avoid the final decision on ethics questions.

Senators and representatives have changed. For example, there is much less drinking than there apparently once was. Former Democratic Senator William Proxmire of Wisconsin, who came to the Senate in 1957, has said that "some senators were drunk before noon in those days" and that, in his first night session, he found that "three or four senators were staggering drunk" on the floor of the Senate. By contrast, Proxmire said in 1988, the year he retired, "There is much less drinking, now; I've seen no intoxicated senator on the floor in fifteen years, and no drinks are offered in meetings with the leaders."[49] The old stereotypical caricature of the rednosed, potbellied, blowhard Senator Claghorn—still seen in cartoons—has long been outdated and false. The average senator or representative, today, as someone said, is more apt to look like a Tom Brokaw than a Senator Claghorn, and is more likely to act and talk like a Brokaw, too, or a Connie Chung.

Changes in the Press

The attitude of the press has changed. In earlier times, for example, there was an unwritten journalistic code that placed the personal habits and behavior of senators and representatives—drinking episodes or sexual misconduct, for example—more or less off limits to reporting. But that code was totally abandoned about the time of the Watergate scandal over the Nixon campaign break-in at Democratic Party headquarters. And, today, not only would the personal misconduct of a senator or representative be fully reported; it would likely generate a press "feeding frenzy" and a flurry of additional investigative stories about the member involved.

Political scientist Larry Sabato wrote that reporters practiced a kind of "lapdog" journalism in post-World War II Washington, that this changed to a "watchdog" type journalism in the 1960s, and that capital reporting mutated again, in the 1970s, to the "junkyard dog," attack journalism of the present.[50] It is much more probable, now, that ethical misconduct of any kind by a member of Congress—whether involving personal morals, underhandedness in making money on the side, or money-for-influence political corruption—will be ferreted out and reported by today's more aggressive Washington press corps. And citizen watchdog groups, too, such as Common Cause, have proved to be much more likely to spotlight the charges involved and build pressure on Congress until it acts on them.

Changes Still Needed

Members of Congress may not presently accept private gifts worth more than $250 from a single source and must report all gifts over $100. The Senate adopted a 1993 bill authored by Democratic Senator Paul Wellstone of Minnesota that would prohibit all gifts over $20, including meals, trips, and entertainment, as well as a nonbinding resolution calling for even more stringent gift rules.[51] These ideas should be enacted into law, as it seemed clear Congress was set to do in 1994. Senator Carl Levin (D., Mich.) and William Cohen (R., Maine) are the authors of another piece of needed legislation, passed by the Senate in 1993. It would amend the presently loophole-plagued lobby registration laws to enforceably require all lobbyists to disclose publicly the identities of their clients, the pay they receive from them, the issues they lobby on, and the congressional members and committees and federal agencies they contact.[52] Most needed by far, though, as is discussed later on, is the need for reform in the present system of financing congressional campaigns, a system that offers too much potential for political corruption, as well as excessive influence by the special interests.

Right now, the most important thing to understand about congressional ethics—in addition to the fact that the ethics of senators and representatives are higher than people realize, superior to what they used to be, and probably better than those of most people—is that individual scandals should not be used to harm Congress as a whole. As Nelson Polsby wrote:

Suppose we were to discover instances of cupidity, unusual sexual activity, and abuses of power among the rather sizable staff of an important daily newspaper? Or a symphony orchestra? Or, God forbid, a university. I suppose that would shake our confidence in at least part of the collective output, but one would hope for relevant discriminations. One might distrust the ticket office, perhaps, but not the symphony's performance of Mozart; the stock tips, perhaps, but not the Washington page; the basketball program, but not the classics department. I do not think that the existence of scandal excuses us from attempting to draw sensible conclusions about institutions and their performance.[53]

We should put congressional ethics questions in perspective. At the end of their textbook on Congress, Edward Schneier and Bertram Gross say:

Like most political scientists, we have tended to treat questions of corruption more or less the way K-Mart deals with shoplifting; we are aware of its existence, deplore it, and would like to see it eliminated. It is, however, so trivial a part of everyday business that it is not a major factor in our calculations. . . . Ironically, the public—survey results to the contrary—seems to agree. Every two years every member of the House and one-third of the Senate must go before the voters. If the Congress is filled with rascals, perverts, spendthrifts, and ne'er-do-wells, there are only two logical explanations: either the American people are easily and repeatedly fooled, or they prefer to be represented by scoundrels and fools. The critics seldom suggest either.[54]

But what about the evils of what is said to be the invulnerable incumbency of members of Congress? Does it not prevent reelections from posing enough of a threat to "keep 'em honest" and make them truly accountable and responsive to the people?

THE POWER OF INCUMBENCY

Service in the U.S. House of Representatives became a career for its members as long ago as the turn of the century.[55] Since the mid-1960s, though, incumbents running for reelection have enjoyed a strong advantage over other candidates.

This House member advantage has been manifested in a number of ways. First, more than 90 percent of representatives seeking renomination and election since 1980 have indeed been successful. Second, until quite recently, the incumbent winner's average share of the two-party, general election vote has been going up, and the number of *marginals,* incumbents who win with less than 55 percent of that vote, has been going down. Finally, studies reveal a "sophomore surge" and a "retirement slump" in house races: the first reelection, or sophomore, victory by a new House member is by a margin that is, on average, 6 percent better than his or her initial winning margin; and in an open election after an incumbent retires, the district vote for the House candidate of that party drops, or slumps, by an average of 11 percent.[56]

Incumbency matters, then. But some political scientists feel that its benefits have been overstated,[57] and others think that the incumbent-advantage increase in recent times has been exaggerated.[58] Certainly, incumbents did not fare as well as formerly in the House elections of 1990 and 1992, both with respect to the increased number of defeats for incumbents in 1992 and the decreased average margins of victory in both elections for those incumbents who did win.[59]

Margins of victory for House incumbents have become more unstable; a representative may win in one election and then get defeated or just squeak by in the next. For example, although only six formerly safe, or nonmarginal, House members were defeated in 1990, twenty-six such representatives suffered drops in their margins of victory of 14 percentage points or more below those of the previous election.[60] And, in the last decade and a half, senior representatives have proved at least as vulnerable to defeat as more junior members.[61]

Also, the power of incumbency is considerably less in the Senate than in the House.[62] All Senate seats are now potentially two-party competitive. Since more of a media spotlight is on senators, and there are only one hundred of them, senators' positions on controversial national issues are generally better known by their constituents than House members' are, which can cause Senate incumbents a lot of extra political trouble. The Senate's greater prestige and visibility, as well as the six-year term, attract more high-quality, well-financed challengers, and it is the quality and financing of the challenger that, more than anything else, determine whether an incumbent will lose. Finally, it is much easier for Senate challengers than House challengers to become well-known rapidly—first, because a Senate race attracts a great deal more free media attention than a House race, and, second, because state-wide Senate campaigns fit and can afford paid advertisements in television and newspaper markets, while House campaigns generally fit only a piece of such media markets, making advertisement in them cost-ineffective.

Whatever the facts about incumbency power are, though, and no doubt the power is substantial, most House and Senate incumbents do not *feel* electorally safe. Why is this important? It is important because of the impression, particularly on the part of congressional critics, that a member who feels invulnerable, sure of always winning reelection, will grow increasingly unresponsive and unaccountable to constituents.

"But that impression would be quite mistaken," Robert Erikson and Gerald Wright wrote. "Even though House members know they are unlikely to lose the next election, they know that their chances are roughly one in three that they will *eventually* lose and be sent home by the voters."[63] And, according to Thomas Mann, members of Congress evaluate their electoral vulnerability differently from outsiders: "Their subjective assessments of electoral safety are dominated by uncertainty—the threat of redistricting, of population shifts, of external events like recession or Watergate, but most important the unpredictability of the challenger."[64]

Members of Congress also feel electorally vulnerable because they are acutely aware that today's well-financed media campaigns, using negative television ads and direct mail, can almost overnight explode some earlier, obscure vote of theirs into a colossal, killer issue. Democratic Majority Leader George Mitchell of Maine has said that senators are now frequently heard talking before a vote about what kind of negative ad might be made out of it: "Watch out for this one, guys; this could really be made into an effective 30-second spot."[65]

What about attention to constituents, then? Do long-serving members of Congress, in fact, "go Washington" and forget the folks back home? The answer is no, according to John Hibbing. He says that when you look at the individual behavior of members, such as their trips back home and the percentage of staff they assign to their home districts, House members "do not greatly reduce their constituency-oriented behavior" over time.[66]

What about the way they vote? Do members, the longer they serve, drift away from the policy views of their constituents? Again, Hibbing has found, the answer is no: "For most members, how they vote the first year is now an incredibly accurate guide to how they will vote fifteen years hence."[67] Without respect to seniority, the most liberal House districts have the most liberal representatives; the most conservative districts, the most conservative members.[68]

Incidentally, what *does* change with seniority is legislative effectiveness. "Senior members are more active, more focused, and more successful legislatively than junior members,'' John Hibbing reported, and he added that now, more than ever, if we value that type of legislative service and competence, ''we should value senior legislators.''[69]

Incumbent Advantages

Still, there is no doubt that the odds are usually against challengers who run against sitting senators or representatives. And awareness of this often discourages good challengers from even announcing their candidacies in the first place.

Incumbent advantages spring from several sources. First, an incumbent is known and has name recognition, which is of considerable importance in a campaign. Most people know or can pick out the names of their own senators and representatives. The average challenger may have to spend hundreds of thousands of dollars to match such recognition. The incumbent, on the other hand, most likely has already laid out that kind of advertising money, at least once, in an earlier campaign. And, in office, the incumbent has kept up a drumbeat of news releases and public and media appearances back home, announcing local federal projects, taking credit, holding town meetings.

Little or nothing can be done about the incumbent name recognition advantage. It is just a fact of political life. We could not, for example, require that incumbents run for reelection under different names each time, just as we could not bar famous nonpoliticians—astronauts or basketball players, for example—from running for Congress. Nor could we demand that incumbent senators or representatives remain mute during their terms, declining to report to constituents.

The value of incumbent name recognition is enhanced by another advantage House members have—the uniqueness of their districts. Nothing in the Constitution requires that House district lines correspond to the boundaries of other local entities—to those of a county, city, or ward, for example. Because a congressional district therefore often crosses or ignores such local lines and usually has no natural coherence or intrinsic reason for being, except that it contains the requisite number of people, it is not an easy entity to organize; frequently, no reason in fact exists for it to be politically organized at all, save as a congressional district. And the incumbent already has the district organized—because, of course, he or she has earlier run a campaign in it, and has won there, at least once.

The average House district is unique in another way: it usually does not fit a television broadcast area, as noted earlier, and often not even the circulation area of a daily newspaper. A House challenger in south Chicago, say, or in southern New Mexico is not likely to be able to afford costly television advertising, when most of that expense would be wasted; the voters would only amount to a fraction of the viewers reached. The incumbent House member in such a district, on the other hand, has the advantage of already being well-known there from earlier campaigns and from being in office.

How Incumbency Became Increasingly Important in Elections

Most observers feel that something happened in the mid-1960s and later, as noted earlier, that began to make incumbency an increasingly important factor in congressional elections. What was it? Some critics of Congress have charged that it was redistricting on the basis of favoritism, state legislatures redrawing congressional district lines after each decennial census so as to produce districts tailor-made for the incumbent House members from the state.

Questions are, indeed, raised every ten years about redistricting by this or that state legislature, and often the questions raised are very serious ones, questions involving equal protection of the laws, civil rights, and gerrymandering, particularly. But redistricting favoritism does not explain the growth in the reelection advantage of House incumbents. This explanation is "clearly incorrect," a couple of congressional experts, John Alford and David Brady, stated, because Senate incumbent advantage trends are, according to them, similar to those for the House, "and, of course, no redistricting takes place to affect the Senate."[70]

Edward Schneier and Bertram Gross went further. They pointed out other important reasons why redistricting does not explain the modern power of incumbency. First, "gerrymanders of earlier years were at least as outrageous as those of today." Second, there are just as many "safe" seats in nonredistricted states as in redistricted ones. And third, incumbent security is not found to be greatest immediately following redistricting, with an erosion thereafter as district population begins to change; in fact, redistricting was a major factor in the retirements and defeats of a good many incumbent House members in 1992.[71]

What did occur in the mid-1960s, and even earlier, was a slippage in political party loyalty in America. This change came as a part of a whole series of other developments that amounted to a kind of "nationalization" of American society—rapid mass communications and transportation, a markedly raised standard of living, much higher levels of education, greater citizen mobility, and increased urbanization. Candidates found that they could go over the heads of party leaders and make their pitches directly to the voters, and they began to do so. Senate and House candidates developed their own personal, cottage industry parties, in a sense. "They ran vigorous campaigns, sometimes supplanting the old party organization, sometimes simply ignoring it," John Alford and David Brady wrote. "Their goal was to win office, not simply to carry the party banner, and they chose their races and ran them accordingly."[72]

Among the voters, split-ticket voting increased significantly: in the same election, a person might vote for a Republican for president, a Democrat for U.S. representative, and a Republican, again, for U.S. senator—or some similar partisan split. Between 1952 and 1988, for example, the proportion of voters who reported that they had split their tickets between presidential and House candidates increased from 12 percent to 25 percent, and those who said that they had voted a split ticket between House and Senate races[73] increased from 9 percent to 27 percent.

As the effectiveness of the party label weakened as a cue, then, for how people ought to vote, the cue of incumbency gained countervailing strength.[74] A congressional candidate's appeal and following became more personal. Challenger nominees got less of a boost from their party labels. They were more on their own, which was a disadvantage for them against a known incumbent.

All these developments combined to make the name recognition value of congressional incumbency worth more. The nationalization of American society also produced great numbers of additional citizens who were more aware of, and attentive to, what Congress was doing and who were much more activist—constituents who wrote letters and made calls, who organized, and who campaigned. There was an "advocacy explosion," too, as noted in Chapter 1, an enormous increase in the numbers of Washington-based interest groups and in the scope and intensity of their activities. And the federal government grew tremendously.

With these added pressures and with all the fresh issues and government programs, the newer members of Congress, especially, began to demand more participation in congressional decision-making. They also had to deal with the burgeoning activism and attention and growing demands of their constituents. They started to feel, too, an elevated sense of political exposure and electoral vulnerability, a sense that campaigning had to be virtually perpetual if they were to survive. Senators and representatives, as a result, made demands on the House and Senate, and they largely got what they wanted. They got more visibility and more subcommittees. They got more staff, more free mail, more paid trips home.

Each member needed more staff and more free, franked mail in order, among other things, to handle a greatly increased load of casework—personal requests by constituents for help with social security claims, veterans' pensions, or immigration matters, for example. Is this a part of the job of a senator or House member? It nearly always has been and certainly is now. Did members themselves cause the increase in casework by going around their districts or states or sending out bushels of letters to drum up more of this business, announcing in effect, "I hope you have a social security problem that I can help you with"? Perhaps they did in some cases, but, mostly, casework increased on its own.

Is casework a part of good government? Probably it is. Somewhere an ombudsman service ought to be available to citizens as a kind of court of last resort to help them deal with, cope with, an often faceless, impersonal, mammoth, and complex federal government. The people have picked out senators and representatives for this chore. Handling casework sometimes helps make members of Congress more aware of the way programs they have passed are actually working, or are not working, and how the programs might be improved.

Can senators and representatives now refuse to deal with these personal problems of their constituents? Not likely. Is a history of performing this kind of constituency service an advantage for an incumbent member of Congress? Without a doubt. If you had been a candidate against a long-time, service-oriented member of Congress like New Mexico Republican Manuel Lujan, before he quit in 1989 to become Secretary of the Interior, you would have heard several times a day, until you were nearly sick of it, something like, "I'd like to vote for you, but Manuel Lujan helped us with the VA to get Dad's disability established as service connected." You would have wanted to respond, "But that's his job, and, if you put me in there, I'll do the same thing." Maybe, but Lujan was already in there, and he had already done it.

A record of constituency service is an advantage that an incumbent member of Congress has over a challenger. Do critics want to force senators and representatives to cut down on casework and similar service to constituents? Do they want them to turn their backs and walk away when water and sewer projects, defense contracts, airport funds, or university programs that might go to their districts or states are being handed out in Washington— pork, as it is called if it is going to somebody else's state or district? Let critics tell us how they would do that. Term limits, some say. But would not the new, replacement senators and representatives help on casework, too, and go after so-called pork just as much? The answer, of course, is yes, they would.

Voters in 1992 elected the largest group of new House members in forty years. But, even before they were sworn in, the *New York Times* reported: "After a campaign focused on fighting the status quo, it did not take long for the freshmen in Congress to start wheeling and dealing for coveted positions in the insider network." The new members, the *Times* said, were already "falling into the clutches of incumbency—fighting like political pros for the committee assignments" that would determine how much influence they would wield.[75] And, later, after these new members had been in office a few months, *Congressional Quarterly* related that they had "turned out to differ little from the veterans," an outcome probably to be expected "considering that 72 percent of them previously held office."[76]

It is interesting that one study shows that the reelection vote margins of incumbent House members do not seem to be boosted by increases in the constituent services performed by their offices, the number of trips home members take, or the volumes of grants and contracts obtained for the districts.[77] And tighter electoral competition apparently would not cause members to reduce such efforts. In fact, just the opposite seems to be true; the more narrow their margins of electoral victory, the more incumbents seem to be scared into increasing constituent service and attention.[78]

Is it fair, though, for members to use travel allowances, staff, and franked mail for political purposes? Paid trips home during their terms can, it is true, help incumbent members of Congress get reelected, no question about it. But do we really want to argue that the number of such trips should be substantially reduced—that members should go home fewer times, stay less in touch with their constituents? Surely that argument would be hard to sustain. And it raises the same old question again: is the complaint that incumbent members pay too much attention to constituents or too little?

Taxpayer-Financed Campaigning

The main trouble, critics say, is that senators and representatives use their taxpayer-paid perks to campaign. But the line between legitimate congressional work and campaigning is always a hard one to draw. Former congressional staffer Mark Bisnow wrote:

[Congress] by its nature is so intensely political that it becomes a practical impossibility to say in many instances where the discharge of official duties leaves off and aspirations to higher office (or reelection) begin. A congressman and his staff, for example, are not supposed to use office typewriters, photocopy machines, and phone lines to solicit financial contributions for election campaigns, but who is to judge their ulterior motives in taking positions, proposing bills and amendments, writing speeches, or issuing press releases that happened to be of value in both legislative and campaign contexts?[79]

President Clinton flies on Air Force One to St. Louis to view flood damage: is he just doing his job or already campaigning for reelection? Doing a good job is itself the best campaigning, both for presidents and for members of Congress, and both would undoubtedly say, with reason, that staying in touch is an integral part of their jobs.

But what about paid staff actually campaigning for a member's reelection on official time? That would be wrong. For some time, now, there has been a low and declining number of congressional staff members who got their jobs because of their political contacts.[80] Furthermore, it is the usual, and better, practice today for congressional staff members who are engaged in campaigning to go off the staff payroll, wholly or in part, and be placed on the payroll of the campaign.

No law requires them to do so, though.[81] And a federal appeals court has refused to go into the matter, saying it involves a "political question," to be decided by the Senate and House themselves. There surely ought to be a law—or at least very clear Senate and House rules—on this issue. House and Senate staffers should not be permitted to engage in campaigning while on a congressional payroll.

Members are already prevented from using franked mail to campaign. For official business, though, senators and representatives can send mail with facsimiles of their signatures in place of postage stamps. That has been true in the United States since the Continental Congress first established the franking privilege in 1776.[82]

Franked mail is not free, though. Congress makes appropriations for this expense, and individual members are given mail allowances. The franking privilege cost taxpayers $85.3 million in 1989, up from $52 million in 1981 and just $11.2 million in 1971.[83] Even with postage for the average unit mailed having gone up from eight cents to nearly fifteen cents during that period, the figures still show quite an increase in franked mail and its cost.

Experts on Congress have found that a major reason for the increased use of the frank before 1981 was a liberalization of the law that permitted members to send mass mailings—such as newsletters, questionnaires, and the like—addressed only to "occupant." After 1981, the same experts reported, increased franking costs resulted from the "explosive growth" in grassroots lobbying. "In other words," they say, "the first wave of growth was stimulated by members, the second by constituents."[84]

A senator or representative cannot use the frank for personal business nor send franked holiday greetings or sympathy messages. And the law says that franked mailings must not be used, either, for partisan, political, or campaign purposes. Yet, a study found that the volume of franked mail in the election years between 1976 to 1988 was half again higher than in the nonelection years during that period. After that, both houses adopted restrictions limiting franked mass mailings (500 or more identical pieces) to three a year (down from six) and prohibiting such mailings altogether during the sixty-day period prior to a primary or general election. Furthermore, as a result of a court decision, followed by their own action, House members may not now send any mass mailings outside their own districts.[85]

Both houses now allot each member a specific mail budget (equal to three first-class mailings to every residence) and require full public disclosure of each member's expenditures for franked mail. This change has already had a significant effect on costs. Moreover, for fiscal 1994—an election year, when the volume of franked mail has in the past gone up—the House has actually reduced appropriations for such mailings by its members by $8 million below the preceding year's figure, and the Senate has frozen such expenditures by its members at the 1993 figure.[86]

Both houses should go further and prohibit mass franked mailings by a senator or representative any time during a year when the member appears on the ballot, a provision included, incidentally, in a Senate-passed 1993 campaign reform bill.[87] And the House should adopt the Senate's present proscription against sending franked mail that is addressed only to "postal patron" or "occupant."

Conclusion

It is true that incumbent senators and representatives have certain advantages over their challengers. Most such advantages inevitably result from the incumbents having gotten elected in the first place and from their trying to do a good job thereafter. A tight prohibition against staff campaigning and the enactment of further restrictions on the franking privilege would expand the potential for electoral competition and thus the greater accountability of incumbents.

But the most valuable advantage incumbents have is their ability to raise great sums of campaign money. Something must be done about this problem.

CAMPAIGN FINANCE REFORM

The costs of congressional campaigns are enormous, and for nearly the last thirty years, these costs have been growing markedly faster than the rate of inflation. For the 1992 elections—with an unusually large number of open seats (where no incumbent was running) and, therefore, an increased number of candidates—total spending by all House and Senate campaigns came to $678 million, 52 percent more than for 1990.[88]

In 1992 the average victorious House candidate spent about $550,000; the average winning Senate candidate, approximately $3.85 million.[89] Including both winners and losers, fifty of the 1992 House candidates spent more than $1 million each in their campaigns, six of them more than $1.75 million.[90] Fourteen of the 1992 Senate candidates, including both winners and losers, spent in excess of $5 million each; three Senate victors that year (Republican incumbents Alfonse D'Amato of New York and Arlen Specter of Pennsylvania and Democrat Barbara Boxer, winner of an open California seat) spent more than $10 million each to achieve their victories.[91]

Where does all this money come from? It comes from those who have money—both individuals and, increasingly, Political Action Committees (PACs), the campaign financing arm of corporations, interest groups, and lobbies. Why do they give it? Not just because they have taken to heart their high school civics lesson about the duty of everyone to take part in politics. Money buys—and is intended to buy—access to power and policy-making. It can buy influence. Here are off-the-record statements on the subject by three senators:

> It is difficult to maintain a sense of integrity and self-worth when asking for money, and then trying to separate that from your decisions.
>
> In some cases, you feel one way, and vote the other.
>
> Congress will listen to big contributors. They have a direct influence. It is demeaning and wasteful [to solicit contributions] and the money makes us ripe for corruption.[92]

The 1991 Senate Ethics Committee hearings concerning the so-called Keating Five (Republican John McCain of Arizona and Democrats Alan

Cranston of California, Dennis DeConcini of Arizona, John Glenn of Ohio, and Donald Riegle, Jr., of Michigan) revealed that they had intervened with the Federal Savings and Loan Insurance Corporation on behalf of Charles Keating and his rapidly unraveling savings and loan swindles. They had done so after Keating had made campaign contributions to them, as well as registration and get-out-the-vote, "soft money" donations for their benefit. Keating, who was later convicted of criminal felonies for his financial manipulations, told the press candidly, if arrogantly, why he had made these contributions: "One question, among many others raised in recent weeks, had to do with whether financial support in any way influenced several political figures to take up my cause. I want to say in the most forceful way I can: I certainly hope so."[93]

PAC contributions are an increasing share of congressional campaign contributions, totaling $189 million for Senate and House candidates in the 1992 elections, up from $150 million two years earlier.[94] "Alarming, outrageous, and downright dangerous" are the words Fred Wertheimer, president of the citizen lobby, Common Cause, used to characterize what he called "the threat posed by the torrents of special interest campaign cash being offered up to our Representatives and Senators by the special interest political action committees."[95]

The Gap between Incumbent and Challenger

Whether it comes from individuals or PACs, congressional campaign money is, for the most part, axe-to-grind money. And most of it goes to incumbents, both because they are known quantities and because they are seen as good investments since they have the best chances of winning. This money, in turn, of course, gives incumbents even more of an advantage. Thus, if you want to know why incumbent members of Congress win, Marjorie Randon Hershey said, "Money is one of the primary culprits."[96]

Incumbents are always worried, and, week after week, month after month, year in and year out, during all their terms, they are always raising money. And they can raise almost any amount they think they may need. After the 1990 election campaigns, for example, House incumbents still had on hand leftover, unspent campaign funds totalling $77 million, a sum more than twice as much as the $37 million that all House challengers, together, had been able to raise and spend in that campaign.[97]

The gap between incumbent and challenger spending has been greatly widening. Between 1972 and 1990, the amount spent (in constant dollars) by the average House incumbent increased by nearly 300 percent, while the amount spent by the average House challenger during that period went up only 12 percent.[98] For the 1992 election, 72 percent of all PAC contributions to House and Senate campaigns went to incumbents, while only 12 percent went to challengers (with 16 percent going to candidates in open-seat contests).[99] House incumbents that year received 44 percent of their total campaign contributions from PACs.[100] Senate incumbents in 1992 outspent their challengers an average of two to one and enjoyed an advantage over them in PAC contributions of nearly six to one.[101] In mid-1993, more than a year ahead of the 1994 elections, ten senators already had campaign cash on hand in the amount of $1 million or more each; in 1994 one senator, Republican Phil Gramm of Texas, not even up for reelection until two years later, already had a campaign war chest totaling $6.2 million cash.[102]

Reform Bills

It is clear that the greatest advantage enjoyed by congressional incumbents, as well as the greatest potential for political corruption, is found in the present system of campaign financing. In this case something *is* broke, and it very much needs fixing.

Strict limits should be placed on total congressional campaign spending in each state and district, and no candidate should be able to contribute more than $25,000 to his or her own campaign. PACs should be abolished altogether (or, if this measure is found to be unconstitutional, should be restricted to contributions of $1,000 for each campaign, down from $5,000). Candidates should get the benefit of discount broadcast and postage rates for the general election. And candidates who abide by the spending and contribution limits should receive public financing for their campaigns, similar to that provided to presidential campaigns since 1974. Party spending, too, should be restricted, and uncontrolled "soft money" should be eliminated.

All these goals are very much what the bill that Congress passed in 1992, which President George Bush vetoed, would have accomplished. With the exception of the public funding part, which had to be dropped in order to bring an end to a Republican filibuster, these provisions were also contained in the 1993 campaign reform bill passed by the Senate.

The earlier, 1992 bill had offered public funding as a carrot to entice candidates to agree to comply with spending and contribution limits. The final 1993 Senate bill substituted threatened elimination of the present income tax exemption on campaign receipts as a kind of compliance stick. The House's own 1993 campaign finance reform bill provided for vouchers for up to $200,000 in federal funds to match individual contributions and to be used for general election advertising, postage, and materials.[103] It was hoped that House and Senate measures would be reconciled in conference. "If you combine the best features of both bills," Fred Wertheimer, president of Common Cause, said, "you can wind up with fundamental reform."[104]

The reinstitution of elections that provide sufficient potential for competition, the kind Madison thought would keep incumbent members of Congress virtuous and accountable, requires the immediate adoption of one or the other of these campaign reform bills, preferably the one that provides for public financing.

SUMMARY

The term limit movement is a mistaken and misguided one. Congress is a more open place, now, and the press is more vigilant than ever as a watchdog over its congressional members and operations. The ethical standards of senators and representatives are high, higher than in the past. Incumbent members of Congress do have unfair advantages against challengers. Some further tightening is needed against the use of staff and the franking privilege for campaigning. But the greatest incumbency advantage is the ability to raise almost unlimited sums of campaign money. Campaign finance reform is greatly needed and long overdue.

PART II

Congress as an Institution

CHAPTER 3

An Unpopular but Responsive Congress

"Running against Congress" has become a commonplace of American politics. A good many members of Congress do it to get reelected. And that practice was also a key element in businessman Ross Perot's independent campaign for president in 1992.

In fact, an in-depth study of Perot's supporters in mid-1993 found that "a deep anger toward Congress" was still at the core of their political identity and that Congress "represents everything these voters dislike about our politics."[1] Those findings prompted the centrist Democratic Leadership Council, which commissioned the study, to urge President Bill Clinton, himself, to adopt a more assertive, confrontational approach toward Congress if he hoped to win over a substantial part of Perot's sympathizers. In effect, the council urged him to join the crowd and run against Congress, too.[2]

Congress is an easy target. Another mid-1993 opinion poll showed that the public's approval of the institution had reached its lowest point in ten years. Only 24 percent of those surveyed expressed approval of Congress and 65 percent expressed disapproval.[3] And congressional approval had still not risen higher than thirty-three percent in a Yankelovich poll reported June 13, 1994, in *Newsweek*.

A public relations expert, offered a contract to improve the image of Congress, would do well to refuse a contingency fee, based on results, and get the money up front. The job of trying to make Congress lastingly popular would be a tough assignment, and political scientist Glenn Parker thinks it might even be an impossible one. Get used to it, Parker says, in effect, because it may be that "Congress, like Prometheus, is inevitably doomed to suffer indignities." In other words, it seems that "low levels of popularity may be endemic to Congress and beyond its immediate control."[4]

79

Why is this? There appear to be several reasons, including cynicism toward government in general, the difficulty of the issues Congress deals with, and the very nature of Congress as an inherently inefficient and conflictual institution.

GENERAL CYNICISM TOWARD GOVERNMENT

This book discussed earlier what might be called the "I hate Congress but like my own representative" paradox. Now, here is another one: the "I love our governmental system, but hate the way it's working" paradox.

Americans *do* love their system of government. For example, a 1992 poll showed that 85 percent of Americans agreed with the statement: "Whatever its faults, the U.S. still has the best government in the world." Only three out of ten felt that the system needed drastic changes.[5]

Indeed, our system of government is what citizens consistently say that they like most about the United States. Because the United States has really had only one system of government since it was founded, Americans may not even clearly distinguish in their own minds the concept of the "United States" as a nation, from the "U.S. system of government." French, Russian, German and other nationalities of people are able to think of their countries as distinct from their current governmental systems. With Americans, the two are intertwined. And that may be a very central reason why we always give our system of government such high marks.

But the American public's attitude about how the system actually works is different altogether. Popular esteem for the U.S. government dropped dramatically in the late 1960s and throughout the 1970s.[6] Nor have more recent years brought any improvement. A 1992 poll showed that less than 30 percent of Americans trusted the U.S. government to do what was right most of the time, and by April of 1993 that figure had dropped even further, to 20 percent or less. In other words, 80 percent of those questioned said that they trusted the government to do what was right only sometimes or never, the lowest level of trust recorded since the question was first asked more than thirty years before.[7]

This declining trust in government appears to be worldwide. According to late 1992 and early 1993 surveys, more than 80 percent of those questioned in Japan had a negative view of their government. Similarly, 70 percent of those polled in Canada and nearly 60 percent in France were dissatisfied with the direction in which their countries were going.[8]

And when people do not have positive feelings toward the way the government in general is working, they do not feel good about its component institutions, either. That is certainly true concerning American attitudes. As Glenn Parker has put it:

> Like most political institutions, Congress suffers from citizen alienation from government. When the [government] is an object of contempt, no institution in the system is apt to be spared from this discontent. Dissatisfaction with government is likely to spill over and influence evaluations of the institutional structures which comprise the government.[9]

Americans as individuals love their system of government, but they do not think it is working well at all. And "the greater an individual's level of political cynicism, the more negative the evaluation of Congress."[10]

DIFFICULTY OF CURRENT ISSUES

The popularity of Congress suffers in part, then, because of the general American distrust of government. In turn, a basic reason for such distrust of government is the seeming intractability of the issues, particularly domestic issues, with which government must today wrestle. As one expert has put it, "The principal cause of the substantial erosion of trust in government over the past thirty years has been poor economic and political performance."[11]

Americans rally around their government—and Congress—when there is an international crisis. The standing of Congress improves when the most salient issues are international ones. But at all other times, look out! The American people expect Congress to solve national problems, and when the salient issues are domestic ones, particularly those dealing with the economy, the popular standing of Congress suffers.

The times are trying, and the issues are equally so. The technological advances of postindustrialism have produced a cruel trade-off, according to Lawrence Dodd—improving the quality of life Americans can hope for, in health and education, for example, but simultaneously eliminating a lot of the good blue-collar jobs that would have enabled people to afford such improvements. At the same time and with reduced government fiscal resources, Dodd says, "citizens must cope with the severe social and ecological costs produced by advanced industrialism, including urban decay and violence, the breakdown of the extended (and now nuclear) family, and the threat to the world's ecological system."[12]

For a Congress that has to deal with such onerous domestic issues, it is hell if you do and hell if you don't. By nature, these issues are divisive and extremely controversial, and action on them is likely to produce "significant dissatisfaction" with Congress, Glenn Parker has said, but inaction is just as bad. Parker wrote: "Since no policy action is likely to completely satisfy everyone, most congressional outcomes produce some discontent. Conversely, avoidance of such decisions provides no salvation. The lack of congressional action on significant societal problems only serves to reinforce impressions of congressional ineffectiveness."[13]

The condition of the U.S. economy particularly affects congressional popularity—and the U.S. economy has not been good of late. The 1980s saw the family income of the nation's richest one-fifth soar, but the income of those in the bottom one-fifth of U.S. families actually dropped.[14] The economic recession of the Bush administration, which helped to cause the approval rating of President Bush to plummet and figured centrally in his reelection defeat, brought Congress low, too.

That Bush-era recession was especially slow to end. Because of it and other long-term and troublesome economic factors, such as the disappearance of good-paying manufacturing jobs, the number of Americans living in poverty had grown to 36.9 million by 1993, according to the Census Bureau. This number amounted to 14.5 percent of the population, the highest percentage in a decade.[15] Growth in U.S. poverty for 1992 was reported to have been three times that of the nation's population increase for that year.

A study for the years 1939 to 1977 showed that when the nation's unemployment rate increased by one percent, that translated into a three-percent rise in public dissatisfaction with Congress.[16] More recently, Samuel Patterson and Gregory Caldeira also reported finding "a very strong linkage between unemployment and confidence in congressional leaders," causing these two political scientists to conclude: "So confidence in Congress—like confidence in a range of institutions—heavily depends upon the general condition of the economy."[17]

No doubt the standing of Congress would improve with an improvement in the national economy. But, even so, Congress would still probably have a serious image problem because of its inherent nature.

NATURE OF CONGRESS

Talk to Americans about Congress, and you will regularly hear a number of familiar protest queries: Why does it take Congress so long to get anything done? Why are members always fighting and bickering among themselves? Can't they, for once, just get together, do the right thing, and get it over with? Why is there so much partisanship?

Congress *is* slow, its work *is* time-consuming and highly conflictual, and it *does* often make a spectacle of itself. But are these not, in fact, the very charges that can often be leveled against democracy, itself? They are indeed.

Public Perceptions of the Nature of Congress

It is unthinkable that a democratic government could exist without a legislature. It is equally unimaginable that a legislative body could regularly carry out its work with speed, harmony, and efficiency. Such is not the legislative nature. And therein lies a basic reason for the public relations problems of Congress.

Congress-as-equine would be a Percheron, say, or a Clydesdale, a sturdy and plodding work creature, not a sleek, fleet quarterhorse, bred to win the millon-dollar All-American Futurity at Ruidoso. The experts know that. But a great many of the general public do not and expect Congress to be something other than what it is. As a result, there are conflicting viewpoints about Congress, according to Samuel Patterson and Gregory Caldeira. They wrote:

> On the one hand, scholars and practitioners who are knowledgeable about the institution admire and respect it as a formidable, influential, and responsive democratic legislature. Many ordinary citizens agree, believing that it is Congress who should make the laws of the land and speak for the citizenry in national affairs. On the other hand, the drumbeat of public evaluations of Congress, elicited in surveys of public opinion, is very negative. To many Americans, Congress is, as critical accounts proclaim, the "broken branch," the "obstacle course on Capitol Hill," the "futile system," a "house out of order," the "sapless branch."[18]

Similarly, we know that working journalists who report on Congress have a markedly higher opinion of the institution than do their editors, the news executives who decide what should be covered but who possess much less knowledge of Congress in general. And, interestingly, radio talk show hosts have been found to be decidedly more hostile to Congress than reporters who specialize in reporting on it.[19]

Still, most media reports on Congress "tend to strengthen the existing negative impressions" about the institution, according to Glenn Parker.[20] Samuel Patterson and Gregory Caldeira agree. They have reported, "Media reportage of Congress, the Senate or House of Representatives, committees, or other institutional components, as well as coverage of members' ethics, both of which accentuate the negative, have a powerful depressing effect on evaluations of Congress."[21]

The public has little knowledge of Congress, Glenn Parker says, and most news reports play right into that deficiency. He feels that this circumstance is understandable since Congress, because of its myriad activities, is a very difficult institution to cover. He wrote:

> The multitude of activities occurring in Congress at one time taxes the resources of the mass media and precludes in-depth coverage of congressional activities. Television coverage is a good example of the difficulty inherent in covering Congress: the number of newsworthy events requiring immediate and extensive television coverage and the amount of television time devoted to national news result in scanty or nonexistent coverage of daily congressional actions. Furthermore, the public often lacks the basic understanding of the legislative process that would lead to an appreciation of the significance of legislative actions. As a result, congressional coverage is usually compressed into a few minutes, and only information that is easily grasped by the television viewer is apt to be presented.[22]

Similarly, congressional expert and political scientist Randall Ripley has said that Congress is "an extremely complex institution" whose "many-headedness" militates against clear news reporting and that "coverage of more than the most superficial aspects of it is rare in anything read or heard by the general public."[23]

There is little wonder, then, that the president is generally rated better than Congress in public opinion surveys that seek to gauge approval of governmental performance. "Presidential news is far easier for the media to cover and report," Glenn Parker again has pointed out:

> The President is a single individual, and policy making in the White House can be described almost totally in terms of presidential messages, actions, or press releases. In addition, daily White House briefings reduce the information acquisition costs associated with

reporting the news. Is it surprising, therefore, that the mass media, like the mass public, follows the presidency more than Congress?[24]

Congress is a deliberative, and even deliberate, body. But its very inefficiency can sometimes be advantageous for the public. Sure, broad participation in decision making by members of the Senate and House, their committees, and subcommittees often slows the process down, but, as congressional expert Eileen Burgin said, "There are few instances in which speed is as critical as commentators would have us believe," and, even in times of foreign policy crisis, "a decision rarely needs to be made so quickly that Congress cannot participate." More important, Burgin continues, the deliberateness of Congress "may counter the often narrow executive decision making and the possibility that policies will fall prey to distortions of 'group-think.' "[25]

The House of Representatives, with all its committees, subcommittees, and individual members, is a "nonhierarchical organization" that "operates very much like a confederation of autonomous units."[26] And the same is true of the Senate, too.

Congress in the 1950s

It is possible, though, for congressional power to be more concentrated than it presently is, and it sometimes has been. Three models have been put forward for the way congressional power might be distributed.[27] Two of them are the centralization model and the decentralization model, each exemplified at different earlier times of the past. There is also an individualism model, which resulted from changes that took place in society generally and then in Congress, beginning in the 1960s and afterward. Individualism is still more or less the model of power distribution that exists in the Congress of today.

Congressional power was said to be *centralized* in each house when it was primarily located in the central party leaders, particularly the Speaker of the House and the Senate Majority Leader. The House, especially, has gone through a number of historical periods in which it was more or less ruled by a powerful speaker—the early 1900s, for example, prior to the 1910 House revolt against its authoritarian Speaker Joseph G. "Uncle Joe" Cannon.

In both houses, the 1950s were a time of *decentralized* power—when the committee chairs, selected by the seniority system and aided by, and in league with, the party leaders, held most of the reins of authority in their own hands. Committee chairs could largely determine when, or in many cases whether, particular bills would be considered by their panels. They could sit on the measures they did not want reported to the full House or Senate. Committee chairs could also usually decide whether or not their committees would have subcommittees with devolved authority and, if so, which committee members would serve on which subcommittees. Chairs of a number of the more important Senate committees, for example, such as the Finance Committee and the Foreign Relations Committee, kept power concentrated in the parent panels and thus in themselves.

Back then, chairs were usually able to dominate their committees on policy decisions, too, and legislation that each of their committees recommended was usually agreed to by the full Senate or House, under a then-existing and strong norm of reciprocity, causing, on the floor, the chair and members of one committee to support the recommendations of another, and vice versa.

Congressional committee chairs of the 1950s, then—in that era of so-called "decentralized" congressional power—were the ruling barons of the Senate and House. As one former senator reported:

> When I first arrived here, . . . you had a situation where committee chairmen regularly supported other committee chairmen, . . . and members supported the chairmen more regularly—it was pretty much a practice. . . . You had the majority leader supporting all the chairmen, the chairmen supporting the majority leader, and it therefore gave the chairmen of each committee more power.[28]

Nowadays, one often hears voiced a kind of homesickness for that congressional past—of the 1950s, say—when it was supposedly easier to get things done, when, it is said, Congress was more efficient. But hold on a minute! Nostalgia sometimes clouds our memory.

Were things really so good back then? No, the fact is that when congressional power was more concentrated in the Congress of the 1950s, a reactionary House Rules chairman, Howard Smith (D., Va.), for example, could almost singlehandedly prevent any progressive legislation that did not conform to his crabbed vision of what the United States ought to be from coming to the House floor. In those days, House and Senate chairs nearly controlled their committees, which, in closed sessions, made generally conservative-oriented legislative and budgetary decisions. These decisions were then largely rubber-stamped by the full chambers.

Congress was more efficient than today, yes. It was easier to get things done then, yes—*if* those in power wanted them done. But Congress was also less representative of the United States in those days, less responsive to the people. Congress was less accessible to all citizens, less open to all interests and views.

What changed? First of all, the country changed. And, then, this change brought change in Congress, too.

CHANGES OF THE 1960s AND AFTERWARD

The external environment of Congress underwent great transformations that began in the 1960s and accelerated thereafter, as noted in Chapter 1. These changes were interrelated and involved more rapid U.S. transportation and mass communications, a much improved U.S. standard of living and much higher levels of education, greatly increased citizen activism, an advocacy explosion in the numbers of national interest groups in the country and in the intensity of their activities, an enormous increase in media attention to Congress, a mammoth increase in the size of the federal government, and a nationalization (as opposed to localization) of House and Senate elections and campaign financing.[29] These external changes were to have a profound and transforming effect on the internal workings of the U.S. House and Senate.

Consider what happened to one type of mass transportation, air travel, for example. In 1950 Americans flew only a total of 10 million airline miles. This figure had exploded to 39 *billion* miles just ten years later, in 1960, to 132 billion miles in 1970, and to 250 billion miles in 1980. In this and other ways, the United States became much smaller, and Americans became much more mobile.

Americans became much more aware of what was going on in Washington, too. The advent of television was swift: in 1950 only 9 percent of American families could watch television at home; by 1955, 65 percent could and did; and by 1965, 95 percent of families had their own television sets. Most people began to get their political news from television, and political news on television is largely *national* political news, emanating from Washington. More people became aware of what was going on in Congress.

The standard of living for most Americans grew markedly, and, hand in hand, so did their average educational level. Only a little over 34 percent of Americans were high-school graduates in 1950; by 1980, 74 percent were. By 1980, too, 19 percent of American adults had college degrees, compared with only 8 percent who did in 1950. These more affluent, better educated people were more attentive to government, more politically active.

And they began to organize, protest, and, eventually, lobby. The Afri-can-American civil rights movement gained its greatest strength in the mid-1960s. In the latter part of that decade came the massive and activist peace drive against U.S. involvement in the Vietnam War. Then the women's movement, the environmentalist movement, and the consumer movement soon mushroomed, also. And so did many other citizen activist efforts and organizations. Demands on government—and on members of Congress—multiplied tremendously.

There was an explosion in the numbers of Capitol-based special interest groups, or lobbies. For example, the number of trade associations with offices in Washington—from funeral directors to retail jewelers—tripled between 1960 and 1986. Lobbyists of all kinds listed in the privately published directory, *Washington Representatives*, tripled also. The number of Washington area lawyers, a large percentage of whom were actually lobbyists, quadru-pled. Lobbying by governments increased greatly—from the National League of Cities to the National Governors Association. And lobbying by foreign governments grew tremendously, too. Senators and representatives began to feel greatly increased pressures from all sides.

Washington journalist numbers skyrocketed. The ranks of television and radio reporters accredited to cover Congress tripled, and the numbers of print journalists increased by a third. The total number of all Capitol reporters rose to 10,000 and beyond, and, at the same time, their relationship with Congress and its members became much more adversarial. Political scientist Larry Sabato, as noted much earlier, says that the "lapdog" Washington journalism of the post–World War II period gave way in 1966 to a kind of "watchdog" journalism that was then, in turn, replaced in 1974 by the tough, attack, "junkyard dog" journalism of today.[30] Congress and its members found themselves more and more in an increasingly bright and often unfriendly glare.

Partly as a result and to some degree as a cause of what was happening in U.S. society—rapid mass transportation and communications; a rising standard of living, educational level, and citizen activism; as well as an advocacy explosion—the size of the federal government expanded enor-mously. Its programs, agencies, and departments proliferated, and so did the committees, subcommittees, and staff of the House and Senate, which helped to create, implement, and oversee them.

Campaigns and elections for the Senate and House were also fundamen-tally changed. They became more national, among other things. National attention began to focus on congressional elections, and these contests be-came increasingly, and nationally, partisan. More and more, congressional campaigns came to be nationally financed, too, and to involve national issues. The costs of congressional campaigns went out of sight, rising to over $550,000 for the average winning House campaign in 1992 and to $3.85 million for the average winning Senate campaign that year, as pointed out earlier. Most of this money was axe-to-grind money, of course, and an increasing percentage of it came from political action committees, the campaign-financing arms of interest groups, corporations, and lobbies.

All these societal, governmental, and campaign changes began to affect the way senators and representatives thought and acted. The external changes caused major alterations in the internal rules, norms, and operations of the Senate and House—called by some the reforms of the 1970s.

A CONGRESS OF INDIVIDUALS

Power in Congress, as noted, was once centralized in the principal leaders. Then, immediately prior to the societal and other external changes that began in the 1960s, power had come to be decentralized, located primarily in the committee chairs. As a result of the pressures created by the external changes already discussed, congressional power became more *individualistic*. Authority in the House and Senate became more fragmented, even atomized, some said, wielded primarily by senators and representatives as individuals and as chairs of subcommittees.[31]

Postreform Changes in Congress

Through the 1950s the Senate and House had developed strong norms, or unwritten rules, of congressional behavior that facilitated congressional action—for example, specialization in two or three main fields by each member, deference to leaders and those more senior, and, particularly in the Senate, reciprocal restraint in the use of a member's individual powers of delay and debate. But as the country changed, so did Congress. Growing waves of new, more individualistic and more nationally oriented senators and representatives were elected to Congress. They were—had to be—more accessible to the public than their predecessors, and they felt more politically exposed and vulnerable than had their predecessors, too. These new members—and some of the older ones, also—demanded more say in how Congress was run. They were less willing to "go along in order to get along," to use the phrase House Speaker Sam Rayburn had once employed in advising newcomers. Individual senators and representatives showed themselves increasingly unwilling to sit quietly in their committees and on the floor of the Senate and House and follow the lead of the committee chairs and others more senior.

These members forced more openness on the House and Senate. Television had previously been barred from House committee hearings and from House and Senate floor proceedings. The prohibitions against television were eliminated. Committee mark-up sessions in both houses—the key sessions in which final decisions are made about bills and amendments offered to them—had always been closed to the public. They were routinely opened up to public view by reforms of the 1970s. Votes in mark-up sessions and in the full House were made public and recorded votes. All these moves toward a more open Congress made the Senate and House "public enterprises" more exposed to popular view, more subject to outside pressure, and more respectful of public opinion.

The increased openness of the postreform Congress aided and was a part of the efforts of senators and representatives to make their two houses of Congress more internally democratic. Power was spread around more in the Senate, for example, by an expansion in the number of positions on the four most powerful committees: Finance, Armed Services, Foreign Relations, and Appropriations. By 1990 eighty-seven of the one hundred senators served on one of these power-prestige committees, compared to only half the members of that body who did so in the 1950s.

In both houses, the power of committees and their chairs was diffused by the establishment of permanent subcommittees and by the increased number of committee and subcommittee assignments for each member. In 1993 a senator served on an average of 11.9 such positions—on standing committees, on subcommittees of standing committees, and on other committees—compared to an average of 7.9 such assignments in 1955. For a representative, the average number of such total assignments was 5.9 in 1993, compared to only three in 1955.[32]

In the House, the members of the Democratic majority on each subcommittee were allowed to elect the subcommittee chair. In the House, too, the chairs of full committees were made subject to election, or removal, by the Democratic Caucus, and the Caucus, from time to time, actually replaced several such chairs for one reason or another. In the Senate, regular procedures were established for party conference votes on the question of electing or reelecting committee leaders, who traditionally held their positions because of their committee seniority. Although no such committee leader was deposed by vote, the threat of the procedure altered the behavior of these leaders and forced them to be less autocratic.

Both because of an increased workload, as discussed in Chapter 2, and because of their desire for greater independence, House and Senate members demanded and got greater staff assistance. As a result, senators and representatives were increasingly better prepared to challenge the committee leaders, and members not on a particular committee were more willing and able to oppose the recommendations of the committee on the floor. What Steven Smith found concerning senators was also true for an increasing number of representatives—that is, that, as a result of gaining additional staff, "nearly all members gained the means to write amendments, publicize their proposals, prepare for floor debate, and attract supporters."[33]

In the postreform Senate and House, rank-and-file members moved to make their party conferences or caucuses their own instruments, rather than the instruments of the party leaders, as they had always been earlier. Increasingly, these revitalized party conferences took positions on substantive policy questions and from time to time advised or instructed party and committee leaders.

Representation versus Lawmaking

As discussed in the Prologue, Congress has two main functions: representation and lawmaking. After the 1950s, as each house of Congress became more open to the public, more permeable by all interests, more a forum for all voices, and more internally democratic, each house became more responsive and more representative. But there was a trade-off. At the same time, each became somewhat less able to act with dispatch—became, in other words, less efficient in lawmaking,

Congressional expert Barbara Sinclair pointed out that the requisites for representation and lawmaking are different:

A decentralized, open, permeable body in which individual members have considerable resources and autonomy of action has great potential for articulating the broad variety of opinions and interests in our society. A more centralized hierarchical body is more capable of expeditious decision making. In terms of process, representation takes time, especially when there are a great variety of viewpoints; by definition, lawmaking requires closure, an end to debate, and, implicitly or explicitly, a choice among competing alternatives. In most circumstances, an acceptable balance can be struck between the demands of representation and those of lawmaking, but it is essential to remember that the values cannot be maximized simultaneously.[34]

Congress today, then, is a much more responsive and representative body than it once was. This change is no small one; it is a great advance over earlier times. But the Senate and House are not as efficient in lawmaking as they might be. And Congress remains a place of continuing, even heightened, conflict and partisanship.

A CONFLICTUAL CONGRESS

Congress-as-athletic-event would resemble the strain, strategy, and "riding time" of an NCAA wrestling match or the shoving turmoil of a rugby scrum, rather than the swift orderliness of a swim meet relay, one contestant to a lane.

By its nature, Congress is conflictual, and sometimes confusingly, disturbingly, unattractively so. This is another reason for its seemingly perennial unpopularity. We say we like democracy, yet we hate conflict. But dealing with conflict, offering a forum for it and for its resolution—these are essential elements of democratic government. Congress is democracy in the raw. It is the very embodiment of democratic conflict, which appears in three principal forms: structural conflict, presidential-congressional conflict, and partisan conflict.

Structural Conflict

Structural conflict is inherent in the nature and form of Congress and results particularly from the fragmentation of power. First, of course, Congress was created to be bicameral, and the two houses are designedly pitted against each other in the legislative process. Then, within each house, power is divided among standing committees and, inside them, among subcommittees. Finally, there is conflict among the individual senators and representatives, newly empowered in recent times.

More representative and responsive today, and more permeable by all the interests in the country, Congress is now more structurally conflictual than ever. Increasingly powerful special interests are more readily able to make their voices heard and their influence felt at many accessible junctures of legislative decision making. More vigorous, and often uncompromising, advocacy by senators and representatives of all types of interests and views has multiplied the internal conflict in Congress and, simultaneously, made that conflict more difficult to resolve.

Presidential-Congressional Conflict

Presidential-congressional conflict is a kind of disharmony that especially harms the popular standing of Congress. As Glenn Parker has put it, "When Congress and the president are at odds, the resulting conflicts have usually been accompanied by declines in congressional popularity."[35] This result has been particularly the case when the incumbent president is an "active-positive" one, using James David Barber's term for an energetic chief executive who seeks opportunities for action. "The impact of active-positive presidents on congressional popularity," Parker wrote, "is extremely significant: such presidents (Roosevelt, Kennedy, Truman, Ford) contributed about 11 percentage points to congressional unpopularity between 1939 and 1977."[36]

Randall Ripley made a related point about the impact of presidential-congressional conflict on congressional popularity:

> The high point of the mid-1960s [in congressional standing] coincides with the congressional ratification of many of the Great Society initiatives taken by President Johnson. The relatively good rating in 1981 coincides with the appearance of substantial support for the major initiatives of President Reagan in that year, especially on the budget and taxes. The lowest periods [from 1963 through 1981] coincide with years of partisan warfare between the Democratic Congress and Republican Presidents Nixon and Ford and also the Watergate years.[37]

Likewise, and more recently, Samuel Patterson and Gregory Caldeira, too, found that Americans "exhibit higher levels of confidence in Congress when two conditions obtain at once: when its majorities are of the president's party and when Congress supports the president's legislative program."[38]

Of course, just the opposites of these two requirements for congressional popularity were present during the presidency of George Bush. He was a Republican, while the Democrats controlled both the House and Senate. Presidential-congressional conflict was pronounced. For example, during his four-year term, President Bush lost nearly half of the test votes in Congress on measures on which he took a stand and 67 percent of such test votes in his last year in office.[39] President Bush swung the veto axe against a grand total of thirty-six bills passed by Congress during Bush's four years. Only the last of these vetoes was Congress able to override.[40]

Considering such a record of presidential-congressional conflict, it is no wonder that President Bush used the word *gridlock* so much in complaining about Congress. In December 1991, for example, he declared that the American people wanted action and could not "understand the political gridlock that too often paralyzes Washington." The word *gridlock* began to be used a great deal in Congress, too. It appeared 130 times in the *Congressional Record* during just the first six months of 1992, Bush's last year in office.[41]

"Good Riddance to the 102nd" was the headline on a *Washington Post* article by Helen Dewar as the last Bush Congress adjourned in October 1992. "Bush blamed Congress for rejecting his initiatives, the Democrats blamed Bush for vetoing their initiatives, and the public seemed to blame both for putting self-interest above the public interest, according to opinion polls," Dewar wrote.[42] The public opinion result for Congress of such an elevated level of executive-legislative conflict was that, after the rally-around effect of the Iraqi war had subsided, congressional popularity fell off the cliff.

But the fact is that a considerable amount of conflict between Congress and the president is built-in and inevitable. The U.S. national executive-legislative relationship is a veritable "invitation" to struggle or conflict.[43] This relationship is conflictual because of the Constitution itself and also because the Congress and the president have different constituencies, different time perspectives, and, often, differences of political party.

We say that the U.S. Constitution provides for a governmental system of separated powers. But, as an authority on the presidency, Richard Neustadt, once noted, the executive, legislative, and judicial branches of the national government might more accurately be called "separated institutions sharing power."[44] In other words, the United States does not so much have a system of separated powers as it has a system of separated offices with overlapping powers. Congress, of course, was established as the lawmaking branch, but the president can veto legislation, and the veto requires a new, two-thirds vote for Congress to override it. The president was made the commander in chief of the armed forces, for example, but Congress was given authority over declaring war and the power of the purse. Diplomacy is the president's special realm, but no treaty made with a foreign government is binding until it has been ratified by a two-thirds vote in the Senate. The president is the chief executive, but presidential appointments to the courts and the cabinet, for example, are effective only after Senate confirmation. In these and other ways, the Constitution divides federal authority and invites conflict.

The first draft of the U.S. Constitution gave the Senate alone the power to negotiate treaties with foreign governments and to make appointments of ambassadors and Supreme Court justices.[45] Later on, this provision was changed. The final provision in regard to treaties and appointments was adopted after the design of the presidency had been fleshed out and partly as a result of the fact that the delegates were sure in their own minds that George Washington, the great war hero whom they trusted, would be the first to occupy that office. The final version of Article II, Section 2, states concerning the president:

> He shall have Power, by and with the Advice and Consent of the Senate, to make treaties, provided two-thirds of the Senators present concur; and he shall nominate, and by and with the Advice and Consent of the Senate, shall appoint Ambassadors, other public Ministers and Consuls, Judges of the supreme Court, and all other Officers of the United States, whose Appointments are not herein otherwise provided for, and which shall be established by law.

Thus the provision for the sharing of powers between the president and the Senate in regard to treaty making and appointments, in a sense, pits the two branches against each other. And the constitutional requirement of a two-thirds vote for ratification of treaties makes senatorial decision making on that subject especially difficult.

The invitation to conflict in regard to treaties and appointments was accepted by the Senate almost immediately after the new U.S. government began to function in 1789. And the upper chamber showed from the first that it could never be counted on simply to rubber stamp the president's position. President George Washington came in person to the Senate chamber when he first presented a treaty to that body for ratification. It was a treaty between the new U.S. government and the Creek Indian tribe.[46] Because of the noise of traffic outside on Wall Street, senators could not hear very well when the document was read, and they wanted more information before they acted. Too, senators were somewhat awestruck in Washington's presence and did not feel free at first to speak out or ask questions. So the Senate decided to refer the treaty to a committee and delay a decision on it until the next day—action that caused the annoyed first president to say, "This defeats every purpose of my being here."[47] But, irritated or not, Washington returned on the following day and watched impatiently as the Senate debated and then finally approved the treaty. Afterward, he was heard to say as he left the Senate chamber that he would be "damned if he ever went there again,"[48] and he never did.

From Washington's time on, presidents have not so much wanted the

Senate's advice on treaties as its consent to them. But, whether it was George Washington and the 1794 treaty with Great Britain, Woodrow Wilson and the League of Nations, Jimmy Carter and the Panama Canal, or other presidents and other treaties, the Senate has sometimes ratified and sometimes rejected, and it has always jealously guarded and clearly expressed its independence of action in such matters.

The Senate has taken the same stance toward presidential appointments. The first Senate rejected one of the names from George Washington's initial list of nominations.[49] And, most recently, two of President Bush's harshest confrontations with the U.S. Senate grew out of this shared power: the rejected nomination of former Texas Senator John Tower to be secretary of defense and the narrowly confirmed appointment of Clarence Thomas to be an associate justice of the U.S. Supreme Court.

John Tower, a former Republican senator from Texas, had once chaired the very committee, the Senate Armed Services, that had jurisdiction over confirmation of his 1989 nomination to head the Defense Department. Normally, the Senate can be counted on to confirm cabinet appointments. The attitude is that presidents ought to be able to select the members of their own teams if the nominees are basically qualified and have no ethical, moral, or other wrongdoing in their pasts. Too, a Senate bias has always favored presidential nominees who are former senators.

But the Tower nomination was different.[50] Tower had never been popular among his Senate colleagues, and serious questions were soon raised about both his character and his previous activities. FBI investigations revealed that he had been a "problem drinker" and an indiscreet "womanizer." Moreover, some senators were worried about ethical concerns raised by the fact that, immediately upon resigning his position as U.S. arms negotiator, which he had held after leaving the Senate, Tower had earned large fees as a consultant to arms manufacturers doing business with the government.

President Bush and his advisers decided to ignore the private advice of the Armed Services Committee chair, Democrat Sam Nunn of Georgia, that the Tower nomination should be withdrawn. Instead, they elected to view Nunn's opposition as an attempted power grab by him and to see Senate resistance to the nomination as an early and partisan showdown between the Republican White House and a Democratic Congress. This view was a mistake. Nunn was a highly respected and influential senator and, in fact, had not been very partisan in the past. But the partisanship of the president begat greater partisanship on the part of Nunn and his fellow Senate Democrats and only hardened their opposition to Tower's nomination.

President Bush spoke of "the right of the President to have—historical right—to have who he wants in his administration."[51] Similarly, Senate Republican leader Robert Dole of Kansas argued that "President Bush . . . has the right to have people [he wants] in his Cabinet."[52] But the Democrats responded with the words of Alexander Hamilton, from *Federalist 76*, to show that the Senate was free to reject cabinet nominees for whatever reason because such power "would tend greatly to preventing the appointment of unfit characters."

Senate Democrats also took pleasure in calling attention to Tower's own earlier senatorial opposition to a number of cabinet appointments by Democratic presidents. They cited Tower's words on one such occasion, when he had declared in the Senate: "The suggestion has been made that the people should trust the President to make the right appointment. I think that ordinarily we do around here. But, after all, the Constitution has vested in us the responsibility for advice and consent, and it is one that we should exercise."[53]

In the end, the Senate rejected the confirmation of John Tower for secretary of defense in a near party-line vote of 53–47. All but three of the Democrats in the Senate voted against Tower; all but one of the Republicans, in favor. It had been President Bush's first confrontation with the Congress, and he had lost.

On the other hand, in the 1991 fight over the confirmation of Clarence Thomas to serve on the U.S. Supreme Court, the Senate lost—in more ways than one.[54] The Senate lost the battle: Thomas was confirmed. The Senate also lost the war: its popular standing suffered greatly.

Court appointments are for life, and the Senate has always shown even more independence about them than it has concerning short-term executive branch appointments. Through the years, the Senate had rejected 28 out of 139 presidential nominees for the Supreme Court, for example, prior to its consideration of the Thomas nomination.

Clarence Thomas was a conservative ideologue. That was why President Bush had selected him. He was a nominee of decidedly mediocre qualifications, too. But the president expected that both these problems could be overcome in the Senate because of the fact that Thomas was also an African American. And Bush proved to be correct in that assumption.

At least since the days of the liberal Warren Court of the 1950s and 1960s, the public had become increasingly aware of the policy-making role of the U.S. Supreme Court. And, more and more, the Senate had begun to take a nominee's judicial philosophy into account when considering confirmation, just as presidents had taken philosophical leanings into account in making the selection in the first place. William Rehnquist, later to be named an associate justice of the Supreme Court, and then as its chief justice, because of his conservative philosophy, wrote in the *Harvard Law Review*, way back in 1959:

> [T]he Supreme Court has assumed such a powerful role as a policy-maker in the government that the Senate must necessarily be concerned with the views of the prospective justices . . . as they relate to the broad issues confronting the American people, and the role of the Court in dealing with those issues. . . . The Senate, as representatives of the people, is entitled to consider those views, much as the voters do with regard to candidates for the presidency or . . . the U.S. Senate.[55]

Furthermore, the Senate reforms of the 1970s and later, opening up the Senate and making it more Democratic, made the confirmation process there more open to conflict and opposition. As Mark Silverstein put it, "With power spread more broadly throughout the Senate and with many more senators seeking visible, national issues to champion, conflicts over nominees to the federal bench, particularly the Supreme Court, [were] certain to arise."[56]

Still, the Senate has usually preferred not to pick a fight with a Supreme Court nominee over judicial philosophy alone, not to decide a confirmation question solely on that basis. Instead, when it has rejected a nomination for the Court, the Senate has usually done so only after finding some other, personal fault, such as prior evidence of racial prejudice or behavior involving questionable ethics or morality. And it was that kind of eventual development, of course, that almost brought Clarence Thomas down.

In the first set of hearings before the Senate Judiciary Committee, Democratic senators had been unable to pin Thomas down on his views on such subjects as affirmative action and abortion. Following a 7–7 tie—in a straight party-line vote, except for one Democrat who voted with the Republicans in favor of the nomination—a perfectly split Committee sent the confirmation question to the full Senate without recommendation. Thomas seemed headed for approval on a close vote there.

Then, details of a sexual harassment charge against the nominee by a former government subordinate, Anita Hill, now a law professor, were leaked to the press. In the public melee that followed, Thomas's confirmation was sent back to the Judiciary Committee for additional hearings. There, Thomas, his White House "handlers," and the Republican members of the Committee were successful in making Hill, the Committee, and the Senate, itself, the villains in the piece. Thomas, for example, in dramatic testimony, called the hearings a "high-tech lynching of an uppity black," as millions and millions of near-mesmerized Americans watched the proceedings on television.

The 107-day ordeal ended at last when the Senate, divided roughly along partisan lines—80 percent of the Democrats against, 95 percent of the Republicans in favor—voted 52–48 for Thomas's confirmation. It was the closest vote on a Supreme Court nominee in over a century. And hardly anyone was happy with the way the matter had been handled.

Opponents of Thomas were displeased with the outcome, of course, and frustrated that they had not been able to force Thomas to state his judicial views on key subjects. Feminists were upset because the Judiciary Committee had failed at first to take the sexual harassment charges seriously. Thomas and his backers, including President Bush, believed that the nominee had been unfairly injured by the leaking of Hill's charges against him and by the process in general.

Observers began to complain about the "mess of the Senate," and they wondered how the Senate could "restore [its] good name." Many believed that Senate confirmations for the Supreme Court had become much too politicized. In fact, though, the president's naming of a Supreme Court justice "has always been politics as usual," as Hiller B. Zobel put it in the title of an article he wrote for *American Heritage*.[57] And Zobel gives plenty of instances from history to prove the point.

Stanley Feingold wrote similarly following the Clarence Thomas fight, titling his article on the Senate's role in Supreme Court nominations, which appeared in the *National Law Journal*, "Sure It's Politics: When Wasn't It?"[58] Responding to criticism of the Senate and the confirmation process, Feingold asked the question, "What should the Senate do?" and answered it as follows:

> The Senate should do its constitutional duty. Just as the appointment of a new justice can change the court, so can Senate rejection. If Washington's interim appointment of John Rutledge had been confirmed, John Marshall would never have become chief justice. The Senate that rejected Alexander Wolcott confirmed Joseph Story. The Senate that rejected John Parker confirmed Owen Roberts. The Senate that rejected Clement Haynesworth and Harrold Carswell confirmed Harry Blackmun. We cannot know how different the law

might be if the Senate had given its consent to the failed nominees, but we can be grateful that it did not, and that in their place these distinguished confirmed justices sat on the court.[59]

No, it was not the vigorous exercise of its confirmation powers that was at fault in the Thomas matter. Senate President Pro Tempore Robert C. Byrd (D., W. Va.) put it correctly when he said that "the 'process' is a constitutional process, and it's done us well over the centuries."[60] Indeed it has, but the presidential–congressional conflict that is built into the process has often hurt the Senate's public standing when it has erupted.

The relationship between the president and Congress is also said to be an invitation to conflict because of the fact that the constituencies of each branch are different. The president represents the whole country, of course; that office has a national constituency. Members of Congress, on the other hand, though their titles are U.S. representative and U.S. senator, not Massachusetts Third District representative or Oklahoma senator, have state or district constituencies.

The result, according to Roger Davidson and Walter Oleszek, is that:

> Presidents and legislators tend to view policies and problems from different perspectives. Members often subscribe to the view that "what's good for Seattle is good for the nation." Presidents are apt to say that "what's good for the nation is good for Seattle." In other words, public officials may view common issues differently when they represent diverging interests.[61]

Presidents and legislators seem to be looking through the same telescope from different ends. President Clinton urged Congress to approve the North American Free Trade Agreement (with Canada and Mexico) in 1993, for example, because, he said, it was good for the United States. He had put his eye to the large end of the telescope and could see the whole country. On the other hand, certain members of Congress were against approval of the agreement—for example, those from Michigan, where the United Auto Workers, which opposed the agreement, was strong—and thought it would cause the loss of American car-making jobs. These members of Congress had their eyes to the small end of the telescope and were seeing an enlarged, but more limited, local version of the national interest.

The president and Congress have quite different time perspectives, too, which is also a part of the invitation to conflict between them. The president has a fast watch, Congress a slow one. As we know, presidents are elected to four-year terms and, by constitutional amendment, cannot now be reelected more than once. Any president has a finite time, then, in which to get things done. But a president's time perspective is restricted by even more than just the constitutional term limit; the greater restriction results from the fact that the chief executive's influence with Congress is usually strongest at the beginning of the term and then begins to dwindle thereafter.

President Lyndon Johnson, for example, was a student of the presidency of Franklin Roosevelt and of Roosevelt's congressionally successful and famous "first one hundred days." Johnson visualized presidential influence with Congress as a stack of poker chips, some of which were inevitably lost with each controversy and confrontation. Johnson knew that he had to get his program approved by Congress early—or likely not at all. Presidents are usually in a hurry.

Members of Congress, however, are usually not in a hurry. If presidents urge, as they so often do, "Let's get moving," Congress is likely to respond, "What's the rush?" True, representatives have only two-year terms, but most can expect to be reelected a number of times. Senators have six-year terms, and they can normally count on being voted back into office at least once, if they desire it. Thus, as noted earlier, the average length of service for incumbent members of the House in 1993 was 10.6 years; that for incumbent members of the Senate, 11.3 years.

Most senators and representatives, then, feel no great time pressure to get things done right away.[62] They sit on a cold January day in Washington and watch as a new president takes the oath of office, knowing that, as the saying goes, just as surely as presidents come, they surely go. And many members of Congress are able to add in their own minds, "And after this one goes, I'll still be here."

Our political party system often puts the president and Congress at loggerheads, too. And internal congressional partisanship has generally increased in recent years.

Partisan Conflict

In the United States, a political party organization does not have the power to choose the party's nominees for public office. The voters affiliated with the parties do. Presidents, then, are nominated by national party conventions, the delegates to which were earlier selected by the party voters in state party primaries or in local caucuses followed by state conventions. Party candidates for the U.S. House and Senate are nominated by the party voters in district and state primary elections. Thus, as political scientists put it, an

American party's nominations are made by the "party in the electorate." This procedure has consequences.

One result is that party discipline is weak; that is, a party organization, such as the Democratic National Committee or the Oklahoma Democratic State Central Committee, has virtually no power to force Democratic members of Congress to vote in accordance with the party platform. Furthermore, just because a president and a senator or representative belong to the same political party does not mean that they will see eye to eye on all major policy questions. This possible division was illustrated dramatically in 1993, for example, when even the Majority Leader and the Majority Whip of the House of Representatives, both Democrats, of course, like President Bill Clinton, sharply opposed the president on House approval of the North American Free Trade Agreement.

Another complicating feature of the party system in the United States has been the declining party loyalty of American voters. Since the 1950s an increasing percentage of Americans—44.6 percent by 1988—say that neither party really matters to them in terms of solving national problems. During the same time, there has been a notable increase, also, in the percentage of Americans who have neutral feelings, neither negative nor positive, toward the two major political parties, and the percentage of those who call themselves "Independents" has risen, as well.[63]

Another way to measure the decline in party loyalty is to look at split-ticket voting, which occurs when a person votes for candidates of different parties for various offices in the same election. This type of voting has been going up. Between 1952 and 1988, the percentage of voters who reported that they had split their votes between Republican and Democratic presidential and congressional candidates increased from 12 percent to 25 percent.[64]

Presidential coattails have been getting shorter, too. When Democrat Bill Clinton was elected president in 1992, he did not pull in an increased number of congressional Democrats with him; in fact, just the opposite happened, although the Republicans were not able to gain enough new seats to give them control of either house. Earlier, in 1988, in the very same election in which the voters chose a Republican, George Bush, as president, they gave the other party, the Democrats, increased majorities in both the House and Senate. Puzzled foreign observers looked at this 1988 result and asked, How does a government like that get anything done? Good question!

So, we get a lot of divided government in the United States, a president of one party and one or both houses of Congress controlled by the other party. The opposite—unified government—once was the norm. The president's party won control of both houses of Congress in all but four elections in the 1800s and in all of the elections in the 1900s until 1956.[65] But the United States has had divided government 65 percent of the time since then, about three-fourths of the time since 1968. Divided government makes presidential-congressional conflict more likely, and it has helped to produce the increase in stalemate, or gridlock, in recent years.

During President Reagan's second term, for example, he was successful on only 51.7 percent of the test votes in Congress on measures on which he took a position, and, as mentioned, President Bush was successful on only 51.8 percent of such votes during his four years in office.[66] "The basic reason for the decline [was] that the Democrats controlled Congress," according to political scientist James Sundquist.[67]

On the other hand, when the same party controls the presidency and both houses of Congress, cooperation between the branches is easier, Sundquist said. He wrote:

> For coherent and timely policies to be adopted and carried out—in short, for government to work effectively . . . the president, the Senate, and the House must come into agreement. When the same party controls all three of these power centers, the incentive to reach such an agreement is powerful despite the inevitable institutional rivalries and jealousies. The party *does* serve as a bridge or the web, in the metaphor of political science.[68]

Americans saw this effectiveness very soon after Bill Clinton took over in January of 1993 as head of a party-unified national government (despite the fact that Democratic congressional majorities decreased with his election and despite his own declining support in public opinion polls). In his first nine and a half months in office, President Clinton enjoyed nearly the highest success rate in Congress of any first-year president in the forty years since *Congressional Quarterly* started calculating such scores. Only Dwight Eisenhower and Lyndon Johnson, both of whom also headed party-unified governments at the time, beat Clinton's record, but narrowly.[69] Clinton won in 1993 on 86.4 percent of the roll calls in Congress on which he had taken a clear position—prevailing in seventy-six out of eighty-nine votes in the House, or 87.3 percent of the time, and in eighty-nine out of 102 votes in the Senate, or 85.4 percent of the time.

Senate Majority Leader George Mitchell of Maine correctly declared that the reason for this Clinton congressional success was that "we [Democrats in

Congress] have a president whose positions we agree with." Mitchell went on to say that Democrats were "all part of the same party for a reason."[70] He made an important point.

Today, the Democratic team in the national government—members of Congress and the Democratic president—are more internally homogeneous, more like each other than they once were. When policy issues come up now, it is much more likely that most Democrats will be reading off the same page, as they say. Likewise, today's Republicans in Congress are also more internally homogeneous, more likely to be "singing out of the same hymn book" on policy matters.

The principal reason for this increased policy coherence within the two parties in Congress is an increased internal homogeneity within the two parties in the electorate. And this homogeneity is a big part of the explanation, too, for the fact that members of Congress have become more partisan in recent years, precisely at the same time that the people of the country who elect them have become less partisan—what might be called a kind of "less partisan voter—more partisan Congress paradox."[71]

There has been a considerable amount of ideological realignment among Democratic and Republican voters in recent times. This trend has been most dramatic in the South. With increasingly strong national Democratic party stands in favor of black civil rights, more and more conservative white southerners transferred their allegiance to the Republican party. As one authority has put it, "rural and conservative Democrats in the South—the old southern establishment—opposed and ultimately defeated by their own national party on the central issue of civil rights and thus 'liberated' to vote their pocket books—began to drift toward the GOP once the Civil Rights and Voting Rights Acts had passed."[72]

The Democratic party's loss of white southerners was offset some by the great influx of African-Americans into the party's ranks in the South as a consequence of the passage of the Voting Rights Act of 1965. The newly enfranchised African-Americans were mostly Democrats, and that was more and more true of their northern counterparts, as well. Nationwide, more blacks now call themselves Independents, even, than identify with the Republican party. The result has been a wide and growing racial gap between Democratic and Republican identifiers.[73]

Each party in the electorate has become more internally homogeneous and more unlike the other in a number of other ways. Income level is one example. The higher a person's income level, the more likely the person is a Republican; the lower the income level, the more likely Democratic.[74]

The gap between Democratic and Republican identifiers is growing, too, on ideology. Those who call themselves liberals are overwhelmingly Democrats; those who call themselves conservatives, overwhelmingly Republicans. The average Republican is a conservative; the average Democrat, a moderate to liberal.[75]

"Party loyalty is now more closely tied to policy concerns than in the past," Gerald Pomper wrote.[76] Democrats and Republicans in the electorate have increasingly held different views on issues, such as social-welfare spending, the size of government, and the amount of government services.[77] It is important to note that the gap between Democrats and Republicans on ideology and issues is greatest among party activists and elites[78]—those who have greatest influence on whom the parties nominate for public offices. Democratic activists are more liberal than rank-and-file Democrats, and Republican activists are more conservative than rank-and-file Republicans.[79]

These changes in the electorate in recent times have produced more moderate to liberal Democratic members of Congress and more conservative Republican members of Congress,[80] making each party more internally homogeneous.[81] Countertypes have been disappearing: liberal Republicans have increasingly been replaced by either conservative Republicans or moderate to liberal Democrats, and, similarly, conservative Democrats, by moderate to liberal Democrats or by conservative Republicans.

The result is that congressional partisanship has markedly increased. The old Conservative Coalition in Congress—when a majority of Republicans join with a majority of southern Democrats against a majority of northern Democrats—has just about become an endangered species. This once-powerful bloc has faded to the extent that it only appeared on around 10 to 12 percent of the roll call votes in the House and Senate from 1987 through 1992, and in 1993 the Conservative Coalition appearance rate shrank even further, to 8.6 percent.[82]

There has been a significant increase in party unity voting in Congress for the last several years—voting in which a majority of one party votes against a majority of the other on a roll call vote.[83] The House of Representatives split like that along party lines on 64 percent of the roll calls in 1992, a high matched only once before, in 1987, in all the thirty-eight years in which *Congressional Quarterly* has been measuring such partisan voting. In the Senate in 1992, party unity voting reached 53 percent, the highest percentage in the previous thirty years, except for 1990, when it was 54 percent.[84] But the rate was to go even higher with the party-unified government under Clinton in 1993—65.5 percent in the House, 67.1 percent in the Senate.[85]

Party unity voting has been even more evident in Congress in recent times on the most important, or key, votes—on 87.5 percent of such House roll calls in 1993 and on 75 percent of them in the Senate that year.[86]

The party loyalty of senators and representatives on both sides of the aisle has been increasing significantly, too. The average Democratic member of Congress sided with his or her party majority on 86 percent of the roll calls in 1992 and 88 percent in 1993, and the average Republican member of Congress, 83 percent of the time in 1992, 86.5 percent in 1993.[87]

As each of the two parties has become more homogeneous in the two houses of Congress, each party's caucus or conference has become more active and assertive. The Democratic and Republican campaign committees in both houses have also become much more important and aggressive, contributing more and spending more to elect and reelect their own chamber partisans. Freed up by the decline in policy heterogeneity within each party, party leaders have become much more active and consequential in the legislative process, too.[88]

In the House, the Democrats, although generally retaining an individualization of power, simultaneously moved toward more centralized power in the Speaker. They granted their leader the authority to name anew, each Congress, the Democratic members of the powerful Rules Committee, which is the gatekeeper to the House floor. Democrats also gave their leader dominance over the Democratic Steering and Policy Committee, which, among other things, fills Democratic vacancies on the standing committees of the House. Jack Citrin wrote, "Under [former Speaker Jim] Wright, the majority leadership exerted substantial control over the legislative agenda and disciplined party members to support their policies."[89] According to Barbara Sinclair, the present Speaker, too, Thomas Foley of Washington, has used his powers over floor debate and over choice committee assignments as rewards for party regulars, as well as an active whip system, to enforce party loyalty in the House.[90]

In both the House and Senate, the overriding importance of budget issues in recent years has also worked to increase congressional partisanship, as seen again so dramatically with the party-line votes on President Clinton's 1993 budget package. On this point, Jack Citrin wrote: "Budgetary issues tend to be centralizing or integrating by nature. Party leaders are heavily involved, budget packages are labeled by party, and voting takes place along party lines."[91]

All these developments—stronger party conferences, more important party campaign committees, more active party leaders, and more centrally important budget fights—have helped to heighten congressional partisanship in recent years. This effect has occurred because, though the American people have become somewhat less partisan, each party's identifiers and especially its activists, the party nominators, in a sense, have become more ideologically different from each other. Thus the seeming paradox of less partisan voters and more partisan members of Congress is explained.

Is increased congressional partisanship good or bad? Well, it is good in one way, bad in another. It is good in that it has moved Congress closer to the enhanced party responsibility that the American Political Science Association and others have so long advocated. On this score, the 1950 report of the committee on political parties of the Association stated: "An effective party system requires, first, that the parties are able to bring forth programs to which they commit themselves and, second, that the parties possess sufficient internal cohesion to carry out these programs."[92]

The increased partisanship that has developed in Congress has provided more party accountability, giving the people a better possibility of holding their political party, not just their own individual members of Congress, responsible for what Congress does.

But greater partisanship in Congress is bad in that it has increased the likelihood of conflict, party conflict, and even stalemate. Party conflict is especially likely with divided government—so often present, as noted, in recent decades. Even without divided government, increased partisanship has produced more gridlock in the Senate in recent years as the Republicans in that body have shown themselves so frequently disposed to use a party-line filibuster against the Democratic majority at a time when Republican numbers are such that the Democrats do not, alone, have the sixty votes necessary to break a filibuster under Senate rules.

SUMMARY

The popularity of Congress has suffered because of a general cynicism toward government, because of the intractability of so many of the issues Congress must deal with, and because, by nature, Congress is inefficient and conflictual.

Congress has become more responsive and representative since the beginning of the 1960s, especially because of the 1970s reforms. These reforms were largely the result of pressures caused by great changes in American society, in issues and interest groups, and in congressional campaigns and financing. The House and Senate are now more open and democratic, more accessible to all citizens and interests. But with power in these bodies more individualized, now, conflict is more likely there.

Partisanship has increased in Congress, too. This development has produced an additional way by which Americans may hold their national legislature accountable, but it, too, has made conflict, even gridlock, especially in the Senate, more likely.

Congress is more responsive than it once was, which is all to the good. There are ways that Congress can be made more responsible, and more efficient, as well.

CHAPTER 4

Toward a More Responsible Congress

Again and again in the fall of 1993, the U.S. Senate's Democratic leadership tried to get cloture—that is, to cut off debate and end a filibuster—thus permitting a Senate majority to work its will, to vote, on a measure before it. But, again and again, the numbers of senators announcing in favor of cloture fell below the extraordinary majority required by the body's rules. So the Senate was once more, as it has been so often in recent times, stalemated, gridlocked, by a determined minority of its members.

On this occasion, the Senate minority was indeed determined. After the first attempt to cut off debate had failed by a vote of fifty-three in favor, forty-one against, minority member Senator Conrad Burns (R., Mont.) declared that his group intended to keep on talking and thus obstructing action by the majority "until there is no blood left."[1] It was a matter of principle, he made clear.

What principle, what issue, was it that dictated such vehemently obstructionist tactics by the Senate filibusterers? Was it a question of war and peace? No. Was it about death or taxes? No, again. Civil rights? No, not that, either. Health care? No. Crime in the streets? Still no. The issue that tied the Senate in knots was none of these. What was it then? It was grazing fees. Grazing fees? Yes, the minority filibusterers were trying to stop Senate adoption of the fiscal 1994 Interior Appropriations bill because it contained a provision hiking the fees that ranchers would have to pay for grasslands they leased from the federal government.[2]

Never mind that the provision objected to was a compromise that had been worked out in Senate committee. President Clinton and his Secretary of the Interior had wanted to raise the grazing fees even faster and higher—to $5 per "animal unit month." Instead, the Senate committee compromise proposed raising the existing $1.86 fee to $3.45 over a three-year period.

The compromise also called for a 20-percent levy on grazing rights subleased by ranchers to others, government retention of ownership of any water improvements made on the lands, and the broadening of advisory boards, always dominated by ranchers, to include environmentalists and other public land users.

Never mind that the grazing provision was only a small part of the stymied bill. The overall measure also contained fiscal 1994 spending authority for the U.S. Department of Interior, the U.S. Department of Agriculture's Forest Service, the U.S. Energy Department's fuel research program, and funding for certain cultural agencies, such as the Smithsonian Institution and the National Endowment for the Arts.

Never mind that the House of Representatives had four times passed similar, even tougher, grazing reform legislation, once calling for quadrupling grazing fees to $8.70. House sponsors, including Mike Synar (D., Okla.), believed that existing low grazing fees on federal lands—one-fifth of what ranchers paid for private land grazing—constituted an unconscionable federal giveaway, an unfair subsidy to what Synar called "welfare cowboys."[3] Joined by environmentalists, House sponsors of the increase also argued that the low fees encouraged overgrazing, thus hastening soil erosion and the destruction of streambeds.[4]

Never mind that the number of ranchers involved was tiny. There were only 27,000 of them, mostly in the western states, just two percent of the nation's cattle producers, but they controlled 250 million acres of public lands and paid the government only $27 million for the privilege. Large landholders, including big insurance and oil companies, predominated among these ranchers, some of them controlling vast expanses of federal lands about as big as a small New England state.

Pushed hard by the ranchers, Senate opponents of the grazing fee increase decided to use their individual obstructionist powers to the limit in this case, as Senate rules permit, and to "take the issue to the wall." In doing so, they were able to bring the Senate to a standstill over what was, in reality, a relatively minor issue and in the process trivialize filibuster use. That kind of obstructionism has become a Senate commonplace.

In recent times, as noted, Congress has become a much more responsive and representative institution. With an end, at least for the time being, to divided government, upon the election of President Clinton in 1992, and with an increase in the internal homogeneity of congressional political parties, Congress has become somewhat more responsible. But it could, and should, be made more responsible still, more efficient in lawmaking.

Reforms are especially needed in Senate floor procedures—concerning the filibuster and other practices that now impede orderly and timely decision making in that body. The committee system in both houses needs reforming, too, and so does the time-consuming, agenda-clogging budget process. Let us now consider each of these needed changes in turn, beginning with certain outmoded and obstructionist Senate floor practices and procedures, including the filibuster.

SENATE PROCEDURAL REFORMS

In a democratic governmental system, such as ours, the U.S. Senate, though "the world's greatest deliberative body," is certainly a peculiar institution.[5] That body was not grounded by the Constitution in popular sovereignty and majority rule, of course. Each state, regardless of the size of its population, got two senators, the result of a compromise between the large states and the small states at the Constitutional Convention in 1787. (And, initially, senators were not even popularly elected, but were chosen by the legislatures of each state.)

Nor has the Senate ever been internally democratic, either, primarily because of the filibuster. Originally, to filibuster meant to engage in piracy. But, by the time of the Civil War, that word was being used "as a term of reproach signifying flagrant legislative obstruction—though legislators knew how to employ the tactics long before they were favored with a satisfying name for them," as an expert on the practice wrote.[6]

Indeed, during the very first session of the Senate, in New York, two senators talked at length to waste time and block a vote on a bill to establish a permanent home for Congress. The House at first permitted this kind of obstructionism, too, but soon dropped it. The Senate did not. There, the filibuster—senators prefer the more polite term *extended debate*—was retained and became institutionalized during the Senate's Golden Age, the age of the Great Triumvirate, Webster, Clay, and Calhoun. At first, the practice was justified by senators on the basis of freedom of speech, which, it was said, was a right possessed by them as much as by other citizens.

Senate debate was for a long time, then, truly unlimited; there was no way to cut it off, to shut a senator up, so that a vote could be taken. Through the years, the Senate's popular standing suffered because of the use of the filibuster, but public outrage against it did not reach the boiling stage until it was employed in 1917 to kill President Woodrow Wilson's Armed Neutrality bill on the eve of the United States' entrance into World War I. Personally incensed, Wilson declared: "The Senate of the United States is the only legislative body in the world which cannot act when its majority is ready for action. A little group of willful men, representing no opinion but their own, have rendered the great Government of the United States helpless and contemptible."[7]

A popular backlash developed as a result of the Armed Ship stalemate, and the Senate was soon forced to amend its rules to provide, for the first time, for a means of securing cloture, an end to debate in the Senate, through the vote of an extraordinary Senate majority. Today, after later rules revisions, that required majority is three-fifths of the entire Senate, or sixty votes.

During the years that followed and up until the early 1960s, the filibuster was employed regularly, but sporadically, in the Senate. In the latter part of that period, it was used primarily by southern senators to block civil rights legislation. But then, as noted, the country and the Senate underwent great changes that were to produce, among other things, an enormous increase in the use of the filibuster and other obstructionist tactics, generally.

Change in Senate Norms after the 1950s

The decades before the Civil War are known as the Golden Age of the Senate, and the first full decade after World War II might be called its Silver Age. Two books by noted journalists who covered the Senate, Allen Drury's 1959 novel, *Advise and Consent*, and William S. White's highly laudatory nonfiction volume, *The Citadel: The Story of the U.S. Senate*, published in 1956, celebrated the Senate of that era as the world's greatest deliberative body, a place of giants, such as Richard Russell of Georgia and Robert Taft of Ohio, and the scene of great national drama and history.[8] A highly important academic book of the period was *U.S. Senators and Their World*, by Donald Matthews.[9] It reported on the Senate as a tight-knit community that had, through the years, developed a set of strong folkways, or norms, which were adhered to by the most influential and effective senators and which, despite the written rules of the Senate, facilitated consensus building, decision making, and action.

Matthews identified six of these norms, or unwritten rules, of the Senate of the 1950s. An "apprenticeship" norm, he said, meant that "the new senator is expected to keep his mouth shut, not to take the lead in floor fights, to listen and to learn." A norm of "legislative work" required members to concentrate on the Senate's "highly detailed, dull, and politically unrewarding work," to be a "workhorse," not a "showhorse." A "specialization" norm, according to Matthews, called for a senator "to specialize, to focus his energies and attention on the relatively few matters that come before his committees or that directly and immediately affect his state.''

Matthews found, too, that senators had to learn how to disagree without being disagreeable. A ''courtesy'' norm constrained them to avoid personal attacks or excessive partisanship. Under an ''institutional patriotism'' norm, ''senators are expected to believe that they belong to the greatest legislative and deliberative body in the world,'' Matthews wrote. ''They are expected to be a bit suspicious of the President and the bureaucrats and just a little disdainful of the House.''

Especially important and, according to Matthews, a way of life in the Senate of the 1950s was a norm of ''reciprocity.'' Senators were expected to keep their word; help a colleague when they could and count on similar help in return; support on the floor the recommendations of committees of which they were not members, expecting similar support for the recommendations of the committees on which they served; and refrain from pushing their formal powers of obstruction, such as the right to filibuster, to the limit. ''While these [filibuster] and other similar powers always exist as a potential threat, the amazing thing is that they are rarely utilized,'' Matthews found concerning the last aspect of the reciprocity norm. ''The spirit of reciprocity results in much, if not most, of the senators' actual power not being exercised,'' he wrote.

How things have changed! The advent of television and the great increase in the numbers of activist and attentive citizens during the 1960s and afterward, the ''advocacy explosion'' in the number of national interest groups and the scope and intensity of their activities, the enormous growth in government, the nationalization of senate campaigns and elections—all these developments external to the Senate and the waves of new-type senators that these developments helped to produce forced very important changes in Senate rules and norms.

Increasingly, from the 1960s on, senators became too impatient to sit quietly and defer to their leaders. They wanted in on the action, the power, and they succeeded in their wish. More of them got on the major committees. More of them headed newly created subcommittees. More of them challenged their own committee chairs and objected on the floor to the reports of committees on which they did not serve. They demanded, and got, more staff to do all this. They made the Senate more open and democratic.

The result was an improved Senate, in an important sense. Instead of remaining, in George Washington's early analogy, the saucer that cooled the hot tea of the House of Representatives, the Senate began ''brewing more of the tea than they're cooling,'' as Nelson Polsby once put it; the Senate was transformed into "a grand arena where a lot of the policy gets proposed and debated." [10] In the process, Barbara Sinclair wrote, the Senate became "more reflective of the preferences of the entire membership and more responsive to public opinion," as well as "a superb forum for the articulation of issues." [11]

But, in the glare of the brighter public spotlight, pressed into vigorous national advocacy by their constituents and powerful interest groups, more and more senators began to shake off the restraints of the reciprocity norm, to be willing to "pull out the stops" and take almost any cause to the wall. The rules of the Senate had, all along, permitted them to do so, and now the norms, particularly the reciprocity norm, had been weakened to the extent that its former constraints had become almost loosely elastic.

The Senate Filibuster Today

Senate filibusters are shockingly more numerous today than they once were. A quick comparison of the number of votes on cloture during different periods of the Senate's recent history reveals this increase quite starkly. For example, only a total of fifty votes on cloture were taken in the Senate during all the fifty-one years from 1919 to 1970, an average of just one such vote a year. By contrast, look at what happened in the next eleven years: there were 295 cloture votes between 1971 and 1992, an average of thirteen a year, and forty-eight of them came in just the final two years of that period, 1991 and 1992. [12]

Two principal additional variations of the filibuster have developed in recent times: a preliminary filibuster on a "motion to proceed" and a party filibuster. Opponents have begun to start their stall, first, on the question of even taking a bill up for Senate consideration, filibustering on the previously routine motion to proceed. That way, if they lose on a cloture vote on this filibuster, opponents can filibuster again on the measure itself—a sort of two-shot obstructionism that can sometimes be dragged out as long as desired. From 1977 to 1982, there were only six cloture votes on motions to proceed, compared, for example, with thirty-five such votes that were taken in 1991 and 1992 alone. [13]

Though not new in the history of the Senate, the party filibuster has only been seen there in modern times since 1986, after the Republicans lost their six-year Senate majority in the congressional elections of that year. Earlier, filibusters had been launched by groups of senators as individuals, most often representing both parties. But, after 1986, under the highly partisan leadership of Robert Dole of Kansas and chafing at their minority status,

Republican senators began to stand together as a solid party phalanx to block measure after measure—including, for example, campaign finance reform and a minimum wage increase—put forward by the Senate's Democratic majority.

The party filibuster proved highly effective for two reasons. First, with the development of increased ideological and issue homogeneity within each party, particularly in this case, within the Republican party in the Senate, the party leader was better able to marshall and hold his troops together for such common action. Second, a close margin between the numbers of Senate Democrats and Republicans—fifty-six Democrats to forty-four Republicans in 1994—meant that, with no Democratic allies and even losing a couple of Republican defectors, the Republicans could still, by themselves, prevent the Democrats from getting the sixty votes necessary for cloture.

President Clinton ran joltingly head-on into the reality of a Republican party filibuster in 1993, during the early days of his administration. He was forced to abandon his recommended $16.3 billion economic stimulus package after four failed attempts to secure cloture in the Senate to end a Republican party-line filibuster. A widely reprinted cartoon of the time—labeled "Gridlock?"—showed a big semitrailer truck, marked "Clinton Stimulus Package," with the president at its wheel, honking furiously, trapped on the highway behind a little car in which husband and wife elephants were riding, one asking the other, "Do you hear something?"[14] In a couple of articles, one titled "A Funny Thing Happened on the Way to the Senate," the *Washington Post* reported:

> President Clinton's economic program was progressing nicely through Congress as the administration relied solely on Democrats to pass the plan, sweet-talking some, strong-arming others. Then came the Republican filibuster.[15]

> The United States Senate has three basic speeds: slow, slower, and stop. In such a place, successful use of the brake pedal means power, and Minority Leader Robert J. Dole of Kansas knows when and how to pump it. . . . Dole led the successful filibuster by all 43 Republican senators to kill the new president's economic stimulus bill.[16]

Whether of the regular variety, the party-line type, or the preliminary kind, Senate filibusters have proliferated and have frequently come to be employed, as in the grazing fee situation, on relatively trivial matters. And the only way under the rules that the Majority Leader can effect a limit on debate is by a unanimous consent agreement worked out in advance. This practice developed in the 1970s and has expanded in use ever since. It permits a single senator to place a hold on a bill, notifying the leader of an objection to unanimous consent, and thus, in reality, to veto the bill's consideration on the one objecting senator's action alone.[17]

As Senate obstructionism of the various kinds rose in recent years, many Senate observers and many members of the Senate themselves grew increasingly frustrated. They began to feel that "teamwork in the Senate has given way to the rule of individuals."[18] The change has "dragged this proud institution into a slow-motion system of inefficiency and procedural imprisonment."[19]

There were other public complaints about Senate obstructionism, too, including, unprecedentedly, those of three Democratic members of the House of Representatives—Mike Synar of Oklahoma, Barney Frank of Massachusetts, and David Obey of Wisconsin.[20] House and Senate rules prohibit floor criticism of one of these bodies by members of the other. So Synar, Frank, and Obey called an astonishing October 1993 press conference to voice their criticism of the Senate outside the House chamber. What Representative Obey characterized as the "arcane and ridiculous Stone Age rules" of the Senate that permitted filibusters, Representative Frank said had "more to do with gridlock" in Congress "than all the other procedures put together." Frank also decried the fact that Senate filibusters are routinely used on such minor issues as "the fundamental right of cows to eat cheap grass," alluding, of course, to the federal grazing fee fight. The three representatives called on talk show hosts and editorial writers to demand an end to the Senate filibuster rule.

Asked to respond to the House members, Senate Minority Leader Robert Dole said that the filibuster had been used through the years by both parties and by bipartisan coalitions and "doesn't just protect the interests of a partisan minority, but also the interests of economic and geographic minorities, including individual states."[21] In a conference on congressional reform, former Republican Senator Warren Rudman of New Hampshire also defended the filibuster. "As for the filibuster rule," Rudman said, "during my twelve years in the Senate, I saw it used a great deal, yet on very important legislation that was truly in the national interest, eventually something was worked out. By and large, major legislation did pass."[22]

On the opposite side of this issue is political scientist Steven Smith. He approvingly quotes a famous U.S. senator of a hundred years ago, Henry Cabot Lodge of Massachusetts, who said, "To vote without debating is perilous, but to debate and never vote is imbecile. A body which cannot govern itself will not long hold the respect of the people who have chosen it to govern the country."[23]

There are those who believe that public respect, or the lack of it, plays a role in the way the Senate is periodically reorganized. It is said this reorganization follows a kind of cycle. Opposition to centralized power (party leader power) causes it to give way to decentralization (committee chair power), which eventually gives way to individualization (senator and subcommittee chair power). Then, as stalemate increases and senatorial and public frustrations rise again, especially when accompanied by electoral upheaval and political realignment, reorganization occurs to centralize power again.[24]

Whether or not this theory is borne out in practice, there is no doubt that pressures for Senate reform have grown enormously in recent times. Political scientist Steven Smith, again, is one of those who thinks that obstructionism "has produced a dysfunctional Senate, one sorely in need of change," undermining the "special policymaking functions" of that body, and that "now is the time to insist that the Senate act to reform itself."[25] He is right.

At the very least, the Senate should change its rules, as Senate Democratic Majority Leader George Mitchell of Maine and the Senate side of the Joint Committee on the Organization of Congress have advocated, to limit debate on a motion to proceed to two hours.[26] A deliberative body cannot deliberate unless it can manage to get before it something to deliberate about.

More central changes to the Senate filibuster rule itself, Rule 22, should be made, too, but will be more difficult to accomplish. The Senate has been held to be a *continuing body*, one in which only about one-third of the membership is elected each two years. This term means that, when the Senate meets every two years to begin a new Congress, it already has rules, and these rules, including Rule 22, can only be amended in accordance with the existing rules. A proposed rules change, then, even of the filibuster rule, can be filibustered, and, to make things even more difficult, a rules change requires a larger extraordinary majority—not the three-fifths of the Senate ordinarily required for cloture, but two-thirds of those present and voting. (By contrast, when the House meets for the first time at the beginning of a new Congress, it is not a continuing body, because all of its members are elected every two years. It has no continuing rules, therefore, and any rules provisions can be adopted by a simple majority vote.)

There is little chance of doing away with the Senate filibuster rule altogether. But there is considerable support for limiting it, and, in so doing, the Senate would eliminate holds by single senators, too, as it should. Steven

Smith makes the very good recommendation that the Senate do most of its business in a committee of the whole Senate, where debate on bills and amendments would be severely limited, where nongermane amendments would not be permitted, as they are now, and where bills would be considered in an orderly way, section by section, as the House does it, so that, once a section was acted upon, a senator could not make the Senate go back to it, as one could presently.

Under the Smith proposal, debate would be limited, it would be kept on the subject, and there would be some finality to votes, once they were taken. After the committee of the whole Senate had thus acted on a measure, the measure would be referred to the Senate in formal session, and there, and only there, could the traditional filibuster be wielded.[27] These suggestions are good, and they would make the Senate much more responsible and efficient.

There is some support for an even stronger recommendation for change in the filibuster rule—by gradually lowering the number of votes needed to effect cloture. That is what the three outspoken Democratic representatives—Synar, Frank, and Obey—advocate. The Brookings Institution and the American Enterprise Institute, in their second report on *Renewing Congress*, have recommended a similar change—the first cloture vote requiring the present sixty votes; the second one, at least a week later, fifty-five votes; and the third one, at least one week after the second, a simple majority vote.[28]

Limiting debate on motions to proceed, requiring amendments to be germane and bills to be considered section-by-section, as well as, importantly, effecting some additional reform in the filibuster rule (and doing away with holds)—all these changes are urgently necessary to improve the responsibility and efficiency of the Senate. The world's greatest deliberative body ought to deliberate, of course, and consider all views in doing so, but it should also be able, at last, to act in a timely and orderly way. The Senate's lawmaking function needs to be reinvigorated.

CONGRESSIONAL COMMITTEE REFORM

House rules do not permit filibusters. Debate is limited in that body, and the Speaker, as noted, has considerable centralized authority to help move the House legislative process along and expedite lawmaking action. But both houses need to reform their committee systems.

"Little legislatures" is what Woodrow Wilson, a government professor and an expert on Congress before he went into politics, called congressional committees. "Congress in session is Congress on public exhibition, whilst Congress in its committee-rooms is Congress at work," he wrote, noting that the functions of Congress "are segregated in the prerogatives of numerous standing committees."[29] Congressional committees may not be as powerful, now, as they were then, but they are still the cells of the legislative organism.

Functions of Committees

One way the committees of Congress can be categorized is on the basis of whether they are standing committees or select, or special, committees. Standing committees are permanent panels with legislative (including budgetary) jurisdiction—that is, the power to act on and recommend bills and other legislative measures to the floor. Select, or special, committees are usually thought of as temporary study panels; it should be noted, though, that the four Senate and House select committees on ethics and intelligence have permanent status and operate much like standing committees, that three other Senate select committees—one on Indian Affairs, one on Small Business, and one on Aging—have had pretty long lives, and that, as a matter of fact, the Select Committee on Indian Affairs is not just a study committee, but handles legislation, too.

What are congressional committees supposed to do? A 1993 study of congressional reform by the American Enterprise Institute and the Brookings Institution outlined their job as follows:

As the basic structure for a division of labor, the committee system serves several functions for the institution. It allows for simultaneous consideration of many important substantive matters without having to use shortcuts because of a lack of time. It allows the institution to process legislation even as it brings other issues, not ripe for legislating, into the policy stream to be incubated, permitting the deliberative process to work. It allows multiple points of access for interests and individuals in society to approach Congress with their concerns. It enables Congress to legislate, investigate, and oversee executive behavior across the range-of-issue areas and executive branch agencies and departments. It creates a means for the development of in-depth knowledge and expertise. And, by structuring committees and creating centers of jurisdiction, Congress can set priorities and indicate areas of greater or lesser importance.[30]

Growth in Committee Assignments

Congress has a great many committees and subcommittees of various types, a good many more than in the 1950s. But, contrary to popular opinion, there has not been a recent increase in those numbers. The big increases that people remember came in the 1970s, and declines have actually occurred since then.[31] In 1993, there were twenty-two standing committees in the House, the same as there had been ever since 1975, and the number of subcommittees of standing committees was down from a high in 1975 of 151 to 115 in 1993. Similarly, there were seventeen Senate standing committees in 1993, down from eighteen in 1975 (although, in between, the number had dropped to fifteen or sixteen in various years). Senate subcommittees totaled 86 in 1993, down from a high of 140 in 1975.

Even so, there are still too many committees and subcommittees in both the Senate and House and too many of them with overlapping and conflicting jurisdictions. The congressional committee system has changed only incrementally since the passage of the Legislative Reorganization Act of 1946. Some modifications were made in the House in 1974 and in the Senate in 1977.

As reported by the Congressional Research Service, critics charge that congressional committee jurisdiction is "outdated and inappropriately aligned to adequately respond to current policy problems," so that "policy formulation is often hindered by turf battles among committees," and "coordinating scheduling among the panels that consider the same issue area is considered nearly impossible."[32] Major contemporary issues, such as health, energy, and international economics, to give general examples, are split up among several House and Senate committees. All or pieces of bills on those subjects have to wind through a labyrinth of multiple panels before they can be considered on the floors of the two houses.

New clean air legislation, a specific example, was handled by seven separate House committees before it was finally adopted on the floor of the House in 1990. So many committees were involved that when it later came time to appoint House conferees to work out House-Senate differences on the bill, 140 House members had to be named so that all the committees in that body that had dealt with the bill could be represented in the final compromise session.[33] Another example is the Federal Emergency Management Agency, so much in the news in recent times following disastrous hurricanes, floods, and earthquakes. About twenty different House and Senate committees have some jurisdiction over it.[34]

Because of the numbers of committees and the inflation in recent times in the number of seats on them, members now have too many assignments to take care of and are spread much too thin to do justice to their committee and subcommittee responsibilities.

Committees have gotten larger primarily because of the insistent demands by increasing numbers of members for appointments to the more powerful and prestigious panels. Take the four most important committees in the Senate, for example—Appropriations, Finance, Foreign Relations, and Armed Services. During the 1950s, when senatorial power was more concentrated, only half the Senate served on one of these four committees, and members of the ruling senatorial elite often served on two, or even more, of them.

Since those days, because of the forceful demands of so many senators, the membership rolls of the four power-prestige committees have been expanded (and, incidentally, members have been restricted to service on only one). As a result, by 1993 a full 88 of the 100 senators served on one of the four most important Senate committees.[35] Membership numbers on the other Senate standing committees have also been inflated in recent years.

There have been similar increases in the sizes of House committees. In 1982, for example, the total number of seats on all House committees was 2,511. By 1992, just ten years later, that total had swollen to 3,177.

The 1993 "Renewing Congress Project" of the American Enterprise Institute and the Brookings Institution calls "assignment inflation" a serious problem for Congress and states further about it:

> Large committees have more difficulty deliberating; they spend more time managing bodies and internal conflicts. Committee hearings lose any pretense of any real discussion and give-and-take when they drag on to give each committee member only five minutes to ask questions. More committee members mean pressure for more and larger subcommittees, pushing the problem to the next level. As committees grow in size, chairmen have increasing difficulty finding consensus and moving from discussion to action. And larger committees and subcommittees mean more and more member assignments, which in turn mean more schedule conflicts, less attention to detail, and less in-depth work on the part of members.[36]

As committee sizes have been inflated in the House, the total number of official committee and subcommittee assignments for the average House member has grown from 5.7 in 1982 to 7.2 ten years later.[37] Similarly, in the Senate by 1993, the average senator was a member of 11.8 official committees and subcommittees of various types.[38]

We can get a more concrete idea of the presently packed schedules and heavy committee workloads of senators and representatives by looking at the assignments of a couple of members who came to Washington at the same time, January 15, 1981—a Democrat, Representative Barney Frank of Massachusetts, and a Republican, Representative Bill McCollum of Florida.[39] In 1993 Representative Frank (then tied with eight others for the rank of seventy-fifth in seniority among House Democrats) served on the standing Committee on Banking, Finance, and Urban Affairs (and two of its subcommittees, chairing one of them), the standing Committee on Budget, and the standing Committee on Judiciary (and three of its subcommittees)—a total of eight official assignments and one chairmanship. In addition, Frank held a party assignment, too; he was a member and one of the several cochairs of the Democratic Congressional Campaign Committee, which raises money and helps elect and reelect Democratic House members.

In 1993 Representative McCollum (then tied with fourteen others for a rank in seniority of thirty-third among House Republicans) also served as a member of the standing Committee on Banking, Finance, and Urban Affairs (and two of its subcommittees, serving as ranking minority member of one of them) and the standing Committee on Judiciary (and one of its subcommittees, serving as ranking minority member of it)—a total of five official assignments and two positions as ranking minority member (a title and position of importance for the minority, with staff, paralleling the majority's committee chair position). In addition, Representative McCollum served in three Republican party positions; he was vice-chair of the Republican Conference, a member of the Republican Research Committee, which develops party policy options, and an ex-officio member of the National Republican Campaign Committee, which raises money and helps elect and reelect Republican House members.

Now, let us turn to the Senate and consider the assignments of a couple of senators, both of whom also took their seats on January 15, 1981—a Democrat, Christopher Dodd of Connecticut, and a Republican, Don Nickles of Oklahoma.[40] In 1993 Senator Dodd (twenty-seventh among Democrats in seniority) served as a member of the standing Committee on Budget, the standing Committee on Foreign Relations (and three of its subcommittees, chairing one of them), the standing Committee on Labor and Human Resources (and three of its subcommittees, chairing one of them), and the standing Committee on Rules and Administration—a total of ten official assignments and two chairmanships. In addition, Senator Dodd served as a member of the Democratic Steering Committee, which makes assignments to fill Democratic vacancies on Senate standing committees.

In 1993 Senator Nickles (tied with four others for twenty-second in seniority among Republicans) served as a member of the standing Committee on Appropriations (and three of its subcommittees), the standing Committee on Budget, the standing Committee on Energy and Natural Resources (and three of its subcommittees, being the ranking minority member of one of these), and the Select Committee on Indian Affairs—a total of ten official assignments and one ranking minority member position. In addition, Senator Nickles served as the chair of the Republican Policy Committee, which advises Republican senators on action and policy.

It is worth looking, too, at the assignments of a couple of the members of the New Mexico delegation whose daily schedules in the Senate and House must sometimes seem like a blur to them—Republican Senator Pete Domenici and Democratic Representative Bill Richardson.[41] Senator Domenici came to the Senate January 3, 1973 (and he is tied with one other person for seventh in seniority among the Republicans). He is a member of the standing Committee on Appropriations (and five of its subcommittees, serving as ranking minority member of one of them), the standing Committee on Budget (on which he is the ranking minority member), the standing Committee on Energy and Natural Resources (and three of its subcommittees, serving as ranking minority member of one of them), and the Select Committee on Indian Affairs—a total of twelve official assignments and three positions as ranking minority member. In addition, Senator Domenici is a member of the Republican Policy Committee that recommends party action and policy and served during 1993 and 1994 as the ranking minority member of the Senate side of the Joint Committee on the Organization of Congress.

Representative Richardson was sworn in on January 3, 1983 (and he is tied with twenty-eight others for the rank of eighty-eighth in seniority among Democrats). He is a member of the standing Committee on Natural Resources (and a member and chair of one of its subcommittees), the Select Committee on Intelligence (and a member of one of its subcommittees), and the standing Committee on Energy and Commerce (and a member of two of its subcommittees)—a total of seven official assignments and one chairmanship. In addition, Representative Richardson is one of four Deputy Chief Whips for the Democrats; a member of the Democratic Steering and Policy Committee, which has responsibility for scheduling and for Democratic assignments to committee vacancies; and an ex-officio member of the Democratic Congressional Campaign Committee, which raises money and helps elect and reelect House Democrats.

The impact on members of their increased numbers of committee and subcommittee assignments was described in a 1992 report of the Congressional Research Service in this way:

> It is not uncommon for Members to be expected in three or more committee sessions simultaneously. Scheduling [meetings] is a problem [for committees and subcommittees], but so are the time pressures on Members and the resultant inability to expend sufficient time in any given meeting. With so many assignments available, over 60% of House [Democratic] majority members and almost all [Democratic] majority Senators chair a committee or subcommittee.[42]

Similarly, the 1993 study by the American Enterprise Institute and the Brookings Institution said:

> The ballooning number of committee assignments of members, leading to increasing conflicts in scheduling, a frenetic pace of legislative life, and a shorter attention span for members, accompanied by decreasing attendance at committee and subcommittee meetings and hearings and less real focus on important problems, has been one of the clearest and deepest problems we have seen emerge and grow.[43]

Separation of Spending Authorization and Appropriations

Another serious problem Congress faces because of its present committee system, a complication peculiar to Congress, is the fragmentation that results from the way that Congress has traditionally separated the spending authorization function, and thus the authorizing committees within each house, from the appropriations function and the appropriations committees. This separation results in a strange and quite confusing system to approve the expenditure of public funds. State legislatures and other legislative bodies commonly combine the two functions, which seems a more logical and efficient way to operate. By contrast, in both the U.S. House and Senate, authorization bills, which usually must be passed before appropriations bills, establish programs and goals and set the upward limits that can be spent for them. Then, separate appropriations bills grant the actual moneys within the guidelines authorized. One authority on Congress has explained the difference between authorizations and appropriations this way:

> The best way to look at the authorization and appropriations process is to view authorization as creating the authority to open a checking account at the Treasury for a designated amount of money, and appropriations as putting the money into the account. Once the appropriations legislation has deposited a specified sum with the Treasury, which generally is less than the authorization ceilings, the agencies may draw upon their accounts, making outlays, which is analogous to writing checks on their Treasury accounts.[44]

One set of committees in the Senate and House handles authorizations—in the Senate, for example, the Committee on Armed Services or the Committee on Commerce, and, in the House, the Committee on Natural Resources, for example, or the Committee on Public Works and Transportation. Another committee in each house has jurisdiction over appropriations—the House Appropriations Committee and the Senate Appropriations Committee, each with its own, near-autonomous, thirteen subcommittees. This separation of the authorization and appropriations functions means that two different bills have to make their way through committees in both houses, be voted on separately on the floors of both houses, and then be separately signed by the president, before money can be spent, say, for a new weapons system or a flood control project.

In fact, it is actually more complicated than that. A total of three bills are really required when the overall budget resolution is counted, as must be done under congressional budget law and rules adopted in 1974. Republican Senator Nancy Kassebaum of Kansas has called this system a "legislative nightmare," stating further:

> Today, effective action by Congress requires a level of consensus that is painfully difficult to achieve. Before we can appropriate a single dollar for a B-1 bomber or a sewage treatment plant, the matter frequently must be debated three times on the Senate floor alone [and the same is true for the House]. We debate programmatic funding levels in the annual budget resolution. We then debate the same issues all over again in authorization bills. Then we refight the same battles in annual appropriations bills.[45]

This system is, of course, an unnecessarily complicated and cumbersome way for Congress to deal with fiscal matters, and one of these three committee tracks should be eliminated. This proposal will be discussed in the following section.

Remedial Proposals

With all of the problems inherent in the present committee system of Congress, it is no wonder that people feel so vehement about the need to reform it. "I think the organization of the Congress is a disgrace," said former Republican Senator William Brock of Tennessee, who was the ranking member of the 1976–77 Senate committee that last reorganized committees in that body. The present committee system is "a disgrace to the American people," Brock asserted, as well as a burden to members, who no longer have time "for real contemplation."[46]

Senator Nancy Kassebaum has similar ideas. She said that changes in the Senate in recent times, particularly the growth in subcommittees, came about because of the "avowed intent of making everyone chiefs and eliminating all the Indians." The "result is verging on chaos," Kassebaum said, so that the Senate "is losing its ability to make policy."[47]

What remedial action is indicated? First, committee jurisdictions need to be rationalized, of course, to cut out overlapping as much as possible and to make sure that, as the "Renewing Congress Project" puts it, "committee jurisdictions [are] consolidated and partially realigned to highlight important emerging policy areas and to create a better balance in the workload and attractiveness among standing committees."[48] Furthermore, the number of committees and subcommittees, as well as the total seats on them, has to be reduced, thus, as a very important consequence, cutting down the assignments for each senator and representative. The Senate should start by abolishing its select committee panels, as the House has done, except for those dealing with ethics and intelligence. And both houses should eliminate all the joint committees that presently exist, as the Senate side of the Joint Committee on the Organization of Congress has recommended.

Major congressional committee reform will not be easy to accomplish. Senators and representatives will fight to keep their power, their control over turf. But, perhaps, today's popular—and member—dissatisfaction about fragmentation of power in Congress and the too-frequent gridlock that results means that the time has come when at least some action on committee reform can actually be accomplished. It is significant that the responses of senators and representatives to a 1993 questionnaire sent them by the Joint Committee on the Organization of Congress put improvement in the committee structure very high on their lists of priorities. They overwhelmingly supported a reduction in the number of subcommittees, limits on members' committee assignments, and the establishment of parallel House-Senate committee jurisdictions.[49]

The best and most comprehensive proposal of recent years for reform of congressional committees was put forward in the Senate by Republican Senator Nancy Kassebaum of Kansas and Democratic Senator Daniel Inouye of Hawaii.[50] First, the Kassebaum-Inouye proposal would combine the authorization and appropriations functions. The same committees would handle both. Second, committees would be reduced in number and size and restructured. There would be ten "legislative policy committees," roughly replacing the Senate's present twelve most important "A" committees, and each senator would be restricted to serving on no more than two of them. These new policy committees would be Agricultural Policy, Commercial Policy, Defense Policy, Economic Policy, Energy Policy, Environmental Policy, Foreign Policy, Governmental Policy, Judicial Policy, and Social Policy. Kassebaum and Inouye would also replace the Senate's present seven "B" committees with four "legislative program committees": Native American Programs, Veteran American Programs, Senior American Programs, and Entrepreneurial American Programs, and they would establish three administrative committees: Rules, Ethics, and Intelligence. The third part of the Kassebaum-Inouye proposal would replace the present Budget Committee with a Committee on National Priorities made up of the chairs and ranking minority members of each of the new policy and program committees, plus five other members appointed, presumably, by the party leaders. There is no doubt that parallel adoption in both houses of the rational and scaled-down committee system envisioned by Senators Kassebaum and Inouye for the Senate would bring about an enormous improvement in the legislative process of Congress.

BUDGET REFORM

The congressional budget process needs reform, also. Presently, it is a maze of incredibly fragmented authority and responsibility.[51]

First, of course, Congress is divided into two houses. Second, within each house, committee jurisdiction over taxation, now located in the House Ways and Means Committee and the Senate Finance Committee, is separated from jurisdiction over spending. Third, as already discussed, spending jurisdiction is divided into the authorization stage and the appropriations stage.

Fourth, the authorization jurisdictions are spread out among numerous committees, with subcommittees. Fifth, appropriations power is decentralized to thirteen appropriations subcommittees in each house. And, sixth, the taxation committees actually have a good deal of authority over spending, too, through so-called "tax expenditures" and "entitlements."

Authorization and Appropriations

It is quite possible that the same House and Senate committees with jurisdiction over appropriations could have jurisdiction, also, over taxation— putting spending and the financing of it in the same hands. In fact, that is the way many legislative bodies do it, and it is the way Congress once did it, too. But, at about the time of the Civil War, the taxing and spending jurisdictions in both houses were cut apart.

Nothing would be wrong, either, with combining the authorization and appropriation functions in the same committees, as already discussed. Congress once did that, too. But, to discourage what had become the frequent attachment of legislative riders on appropriations bills, both houses separated those functions as well as the committees responsible for them. Still, until the end of World War II, most agencies and programs of the federal government were authorized on a permanent basis. Since then, it has become the practice to vote authorizations for shorter and shorter periods, and now they are usually for no more than a year or two in duration.

Back when the appropriations power was first taken away from the taxation committees, it was initially divided among several separate committees in each house. Later on, that power was reconcentrated in two appropriations committees. Still later, it was split up again among about nine committees in each house and then reconcentrated once more in two appropriations committees. These two committees were themselves eventually divided into largely autonomous subcommittees, presently thirteen each, as already noted.

The basic jurisdictions of the two committees that deal with taxation— the Ways and Means Committee in the House and the Finance Committee in the Senate—have been expanded through the years to include authority over more than half of all federal spending through the enactment of entitlements and tax expenditures. Social Security benefits and, later, those under Medicare were created as rights, as entitlements, for all those who met the qualifications set by law. No annual or biennial authorizations for Social Security and Medicare are necessary; the government pays for all those who are eligible, whatever the cost. The fact that these programs are funded by earmarked taxes is the reason that the Ways and Means Committee and the Finance Committee, not the authorizing and appropriating committees, have jurisdiction over them. And Medicaid, medical assistance for the poor, though funded out of general revenue, is also treated as an entitlement and comes within the jurisdiction of the two taxation committees.

Tax expenditures came about when, in situation after situation, Congress decided to encourage certain behavior by giving a tax break for it. For example, it encourages investment in municipal bonds by exempting interest on them from taxation and investment in rental property by granting deductions from rental income for depreciation expense and allowing operating losses from such activity in certain cases to be deducted for tax purposes from income from other sources.

The impact on the federal treasury of these and similar tax incentives is the same as if the full amount of the taxes that would otherwise be owed were collected and then handed back to the relevant citizens as a cash subsidy; that is why they are called tax expenditures. In the latter case, though, not the taxation committees, but the authorizing and appropriating committees would have had jurisdiction. Furthermore, outright subsidies would have had to be regularly reauthorized and reappropriated for, which is not required for tax expenditures. Tax expenditures now run into the billions of dollars and continue in force until the law is changed or they are repealed.

No wonder the recipients of tax expenditures like that method of handling incentives. And no wonder, either, that Republicans in Congress have been the strongest supporters of tax expenditures, while congressional Democrats have been the strongest backers of entitlements. As Howard Shuman, an authority on the federal budget process, wrote:

> There is a political schizophrenia between those who favor tax
> expenditures but oppose spending expenditures and those who defend
> spending expenditures but oppose tax expenditures. The reason why
> this division exists is relatively simple, if unstated. It is partisan and
> political. Tax [expenditures] . . . generally benefit those with higher
> incomes. The poor, who pay no income taxes, only casually or by
> serendipity receive tax expenditures.[52]

Failures of the 1974 Reform

In any event, entitlements and tax expenditures further fragment congressional authority over spending, which was already, as noted, practically in splinters. To provide some coherence in the budget process—at least that was a major reason—Congress adopted the Budget and Impoundment Control Act of 1974.[53]

Another purpose of this act was to prevent the president from impounding—that is, refusing to spend—money appropriated by Congress for specific purposes. The new law worked in that respect in just the way Congress expected. But that was hardly the case for the other goals of the 1974 budget reform.

Liberal backers of the act had been concerned about rapidly growing federal deficits, which were up alarmingly, they thought, from an average of $11.7 billion during each of President Richard Nixon's first two fiscal years to an average of $63.5 billion during the last two. Of course, the deficit levels of the years prior to the budget reform act of 1974 looked mighty small indeed later on, after the annual deficits of the Reagan era and afterward shot up to the $200 billion range and even beyond.

Nor did the hope of the liberal backers of the budget reform act of 1974 that it would change federal priorities and reduce military spending prove out in practice. Military appropriations skyrocketed under President Ronald Reagan, while social spending was reduced as a percentage of the gross national product. There was no realization, either, of the hope for better management of fiscal policy—countercyclical use by Congress of its spending and taxing powers to ameliorate economic booms and busts that produce rising unemployment or rising inflation.

Neither did the 1974 reform simplify the congressional budget process. In fact, it made it more complicated. The dichotomy between authorizing and appropriating was not dealt with at all. Instead, a new layer of authority and procedure was imposed on the old: the act created a House Budget Committee and a Senate Budget Committee, as well as an expertly staffed Congressional Budget Office (CBO) to advise them and Congress, and it mandated two-step budget committee and congressional action: in May of each year, a tentative overall budget, which was to be advisory, when adopted, for the taxation, authorizing, and appropriations committees and a final budget in September, which was to be binding on all the committees, once enacted.

The CBO did a good job from the start, giving Congress, for the first time, and reliably, the ability to make its own economic forecasts and resultant revenue and spending estimates. And, at first, the budgeting process worked pretty well, on a largely nonpartisan basis, though the first advisory budget resolution was abandoned after a while.

Then came the Reagan earthquake that tore up the economic and fiscal landscape:[54] a recommended and massive tax cut, which wiser heads in Congress could neither politically withstand nor procedurally forestall; a huge military build-up, fueled by a heightened Soviet scare; and resultant leaps in annual deficits, worsened greatly when revenues dropped and welfare-type costs surged as a consequence of an especially harsh tight-money recession instituted by the Federal Reserve with Reagan administration approval.[55]

Nobody had ever dreamed, or had nightmares about, deficits at the levels that the country then began to experience. The public was frightened, and so was Congress. Indications were that both a popular and a congressional majority might support a tax increase to deal with the deficits, but President Reagan declared that if Congress passed such a measure, it would be dead *before* arrival. There was no way Congress could increase taxes.

Public opinion was in favor of cutting military expenditures. But President Reagan vowed to stop that type of deficit reduction action, also. He agreed with Congress that entitlements should not be cut. And nearly everyone was of the opinion that social spending had already been reduced as far as was prudent. Still, the public, the president, and Congress were all shouting with one voice: cut the deficits!

How? It was at that moment that, without committee hearings, the Senate adopted the Gramm-Rudman-Hollings measure as an amendment to a pending debt-ceiling bill. It provided for automatic and mandatory, across-the-board spending cuts each year for five years (with certain exceptions, such as those for poverty programs and defense contracts), if Congress, itself, did not vote the cuts, until the deficit was, in regular steps, reduced inexorably to zero, or so it was hoped.[56] One senator at the time called Gramm-Rudman-Hollings a fraudulent evasion of responsibility and a "fiscal straitjacket" and declared that its enactment was the same as Congress saying, "Stop me before I kill again."[57]

Reform Proposals

The Gramm-Rudman-Hollings law did operate as a restraint on what congressional spending might otherwise have been. But it did not work to eliminate the deficits. Congress periodically passed laws changing the target year for zeroing them out. Neither did the law cut down on the great number of budget votes that had begun to be taken to the floor, especially in the Senate, after passage of the 1974 budget reform, nor did it lower the high degree of partisanship that had come to polarize all budget battles in Congress.

A bipartisan, presidential-congressional budget summit, and its multiple-year budget, were key accomplishments of the last part of the Bush administration, though the concomitant abandonment of Bush's "read my lips" campaign promise of no new taxes proved fatally damaging to both his public standing and his reelection hopes.[58] President Clinton did not hold a budget summit with Congress, and he should have, but his recommended multiple-year budget bill, which passed the House and Senate during Clinton's first year in office in 1993, was an even greater accomplishment than that of Bush and was predicted to reduce the federal deficit over five years by $496 billion.[59] The Clinton budget package finally passed in both the Senate and House without a single vote to spare, in the Senate after Vice-President Al Gore broke a 50–50 tie to make the vote a bare 51–50 and in the House by a vote of 218–216 after a first-year Democratic legislator gave in to White House pleas and voted with the president, thus preventing the measure's loss on a 217–217 tie (one of the 435 House seats being vacant at the time because of a death). And in both houses, too, the Clinton budget deal was adopted on a straight party-line vote, without a single Republican supporting it, the first time since World War II, and maybe the first time ever, that the majority party in Congress had passed a major piece of legislation without getting even one vote from the opposition.

The only reason President Clinton was able to secure adoption of his budget package under such circumstances was that in earlier years the Senate had adopted restraints on debate that apply solely to the budget reconciliation resolution. Debate on it is limited to twenty hours, so that there can be no filibustering of the resolution, and amendments to it must be germane.[60] If such restraints are good enough for the Senate's budget process, why are they not good enough to be applied to the rest of the floor action in that body?

There is widespread belief that the budget process of Congress is out of whack and ought to be reformed. Needed reforms fall into three categories: institutionalized budget summits, multiyear budgeting, and committee reform.

Since the first budget resolution contemplated by the 1974 budget reform law has now been eliminated, and everything is presently crammed into the one binding reconciliation resolution, there is a special premium on early, high-level House-Senate and congressional-presidential budget negotiations.

The first budget summit ever was the Reagan summit of 1987. It worked. As Democratic Senator J. Bennett Johnston of Louisiana said: "The ad hoc budget summit of last year [1987] had all the principals, plus the White House, and came up with the parameters and exact numbers. Consequently, we'll have [all] thirteen appropriations bills on the President's desk in October of this year [1988], the first time since 1948. This is the prototype, with the right people."[61]

Indeed, the 1987 Reagan summit did prove to be the prototype for the Bush summit that followed it in 1990. That one worked, too. And there was a good chance in 1993 that President Clinton might have been able to avoid hairbreadth Senate and House vote margins and pick up some Republican support for his multiyear budget package, or something close to it, had he involved senators and representatives of that party from the first in the production of the package.

The ranking member of the Senate Budget Committee, Senator Pete Domenici (R., N.M.) made the case for institutionalized budget summits, as well as multiyear budgeting, when he said: "We need a two-year budget— with a joint committee, leadership-appointed, in the first ninety days of the first year [of each Congress]. This would work very much like the [Reagan] summit, but with more meat on the bones."[62]

Domenici's suggestion called for a summit made up of the party leaders and the leaders of both parties of the two budget committees of the House and Senate, the two appropriations committees, and the two taxation committees, as well as the relevant officials from the executive branch. The institutionalization of such a device would provide a permanent mechanism for arching over our national government's branch, house, and party divisions.

There is overwhelming support for multiyear budgeting, resulting from the budget packages adopted after the Reagan summit of 1987 and the Bush summit of 1990 as well as from, of course, passage of the Clinton budget package in 1993. Congress has three times endorsed the concept in practice.

The 1993 report of the Joint Committee on the Organization of Congress recommended multiyear budgeting, too, calling for regular budgeting on a two-year basis.[63] This longer-term budgeting ought to be adopted as the rule in Congress, with the first year of a Congress devoted to the budget and the second year to authorizations and oversight.

And, of course, congressional committees must be realigned. There is very strong support for eliminating one of the three committee levels in the budget process—authorization, appropriations, and budget—though there is great disagreement about which one. The best proposal, again, is that recommended by Senators Kassebaum and Inouye, combining the authorization and appropriation functions in the same realigned and reduced number of committees, with the leaders of them, as well as the party and other leaders, to comprise a National Priorities Committee that would replace the budget committees in each house. These committees, if established in the House and Senate, could function as the congressional part of an institutionalized budget summit, too.

The Kassebaum-Inouye proposal would help to make sense out of a presently messy and disorderly budget process and would make Congress more responsible concerning budget decisions, more able to act in a timely and orderly way in respect to them.

SUMMARY

Congress is, by and large, a responsive and representative institution. It can and should be made more responsible and efficient. Since Senate norms that facilitated action have been relaxed in recent years, the rules of that body that make timely action difficult, especially the rules about the filibuster and germaneness of floor amendments, are greatly in need of change. Committees in both houses should be realigned and reduced in number. The number of subcommittees should be reduced, too. The assignments of senators and representatives to committees and subcommittees should be cut back. And the budget process should be modernized, through institutionalized budget summits, multiyear budgeting, and committee realignment.

All these needed reforms would go a long way toward making Congress as responsible as it is responsive.

Epilogue

What would America do without Congress? That question is posed by Edward Schneier and Bertram Gross in their book *Congress Today*. Here is the way they answer:

> Humorists would be in trouble. Secrecy would be compounded. Dedicated civil servants would lose one major way to break through bureaucratic or special-interest obstructionism. The "best and the brightest" of all the great experts would conduct their squabbles in greater secrecy and with less sense of social responsibility. There would be fewer policy innovations.[1]

The part about the humorists losing a lot of material is most certainly true. And the Congress-bashers would be bereft, also.

Congress is, as we have seen, both a gathering of individuals and an organization, or institution. We like our own members of Congress because we believe that they do well at what we expect of them—serving as our advocates, representing our interests. But we have a rather low regard for all those *other* representatives of somebody else.

It is wrong and unfair to charge, as critics do, that what members of Congress cost us is extravagant and skyrocketing. That is simply not true. If we compare the cost of Congress with the size of the federal government that they must oversee and how the government has grown so enormously or if we compare the price we pay for Congress with the cost of other national legislatures, given, particularly, that most of them, in parliamentary systems, have a much less independent and vital role, these comparisons show that the costs of Congress are not excessive. Nor are they swelling; to the contrary, congressional costs stayed virtually the same in constant dollars during the last decade or more, and they are recently being rolled back some.

Member salaries. The salaries of members of Congress are not exorbitant, either, though, through history and into the present, demagogic appeals on this issue have proved easy to make to people who earn a good deal less than senators and representatives do. An unpaid, volunteer national legislature would be an unrepresentative one, since even fewer people without great means would be able to serve there. And to pay senators and representatives less than what is necessary for them to live on would be to encourage their serving two masters, us and the special interests who would be only too glad to help them make ends meet. Or it would force members, as it once did, to split their attention between the public's business and their own, running a law practice or engaging in some other private money-making activity on the side.

It is, of course, a built-in political embarrassment for members of Congress to have to decide on the amount of their own salaries, a two-hundred year dilemma for them. But there is no way around this; Congress controls the federal purse strings. And the present salary that members have set is in line with the high level of professionalism required of them today, with the salaries of other national legislators, with their tremendous responsibilities, with the difficulty and financial drain of their jobs, and with the pay of comparable public and private positions.

Perks and privileges.   Congress should, as it is apparently poised to do, apply to itself all the laws it has enacted to cover executive department and private employers. But complaints about the perks and privileges of members of Congress mostly amount to paltry carping or gross overstatement, whether they have to do with Capitol restaurants, barber shops, gymnasiums, or the like. Senators and representatives are not living cloistered, lavish lives, enjoying unjustified emoluments of office, at taxpayer expense.

The so-called House bank scandal that so badly injured the image of Congress was a shamefully overreported, Republican-lit, and talk-show-host–fanned promotional fire. It did not have to do with a real bank, did not lose any taxpayer money, and, even with a special outside prosecutor, did not turn up a bunch of congressional crooks, as promised. The practices at the bank in honoring overdrafts, often without notice to members, had been sloppy, and the bank has been abolished.

Staff growth.   It seems that everybody, including some members themselves, likes to jump on Congress for having too much staff—"bloated" is the modifier most often used when congressional staff is mentioned. It was an advocacy explosion in the numbers of national interest groups and the intensity of their activities, as well as an enormous growth in government, with the resultant increase in the size and complexity of members' jobs that these developments produced, that caused members of Congress to expand the numbers of their own personnel that they could look to for reliable advice and help. Not to have done so would have been to cede permanently a good portion of their constitutional responsibilities to the bureaucrats and the executive branch and to have handed an advantage to the special interests and the lobbyists who work for them.

Congress-bashers are wrong, too, in claiming that the growth of staff numbers continues to surge. It does not. Still, responding to criticism, both houses have moved to cut back some on staff. But they must be careful not to cut for cutting's sake and in the process reduce their own autonomy and independence and reconcentrate power in too few hands internally.

Term limits.   An open and transparent Congress, one in which people can see what is going on, which is more and more what Congress has become, as well as free and competitive elections, as James Madison knew, are the best means for holding members of Congress accountable. Not term limits. The Founders were right in rejecting term limits, because to do otherwise would be to restrict unreasonably the power of the people; to take away the hope of reelection, one of the important incentives for good conduct in office; and to deny public service to those most experienced in it.

It is highly likely that state attempts to impose congressional term limits will be held to be in violation of the U.S. Constitution in that they would add another qualification to those already required. And, in any event, most such plans would not produce turnover substantially different from that of the present turnover, occasioned by deaths, defeats, and voluntary retirements. Limiting the terms of members of Congress would further empower the bureaucrats and lobbyists whose time in Washington, of course, is open ended.

Member ethics.   But what can be done, then, about the ethics of incumbent senators and representatives? In the first place, by all accounts, the ethics of members of Congress are high, higher than ever. Yes, but what about all that we read concerning the sexual misconduct of Republican Senator Robert Packwood of Oregon, for example, or the ongoing investigation of the dealings of the now-deposed former chairman of the House Ways and Means Committee, Illinois Democrat Daniel Rostenkowski, with the House post office?

First, it is noteworthy that we *have* heard about these cases. Once, we might not have. Once, neither the House nor the Senate was subject to clear and tough standards of ethics and laws about member conduct, nor were there any good and workable means of dealing with transgressions. Now there are both.

Senators and representatives who are investigated and censured or repri-

manded by their parent body either quit or get beat. Notice that the three
members of the Keating Five who got the strongest Senate Ethics Committee
rebukes for assisting savings and loan crook Charles Keating after accepting
his campaign help have already eschewed reelection, as in the case of Alan
Cranston (D., Calif.), who would have been up in 1992, and Democrats
Dennis DeConcini of Arizona and Donald E. Riegle, Jr., of Michigan, whose
terms were set to expire in 1994.[2]

Senators and representatives cannot practice law, now, on the side.
They cannot hire their relatives. They cannot accept so-called "honoraria" from interest groups or others. Gift laws should be tightened
further, as Congress was set to do in 1994, and so should lobby registration laws. But the greatest remaining threat to congressional ethics is
the way we finance campaigns for the Senate and House, which should be
reformed.

Incumbent members of Congress have a good many very important
advantages that their challengers do not enjoy. Inevitably, doing a good job
in office is good politics, too. House members, especially, who enjoy more
of an advantage of incumbency than senators, have the benefit of the odds
over challengers in a number of ways: because they have name recognition,
from both earlier campaigning and from being in office; because of the
opportunity to build a record of constituency service; because of certain
perks of office, such as staff and free mail; and because their districts are
unique, not usually fitting governmental unit lines or broadcast markets, and
are, therefore, difficult for challengers to organize, while incumbents already
have them organized. Furthermore, as party loyalty has declined in recent
times, and thus the power of the cue of the party label for voters has decreased, too, incumbency loyalty has correspondingly, and resultingly,
climbed.

Congressional staff, of course, should not be used for campaigning, and
franked mail should be further curtailed, particularly to prohibit mass franked
mailings by a senator or representative during a year when the member
appears on the ballot and, in the House, to outlaw altogether franked mail
addressed to "postal patron" or "occupant," as the Senate has already
done. But the way campaigns are financed constitutes the greatest incumbent
advantage. Reforming this system would not only improve the ethical climate
of Congress, but would also help to make congressional elections more
competitive and members, thus, more accountable.

Campaign costs.   The campaign costs for getting elected or reelected
to the Senate and House are enormous and growing. The money comes from

people who expect something in return, whether it comes from individuals or political action committees (PACs), the campaign-financing arm of interest groups, lobbies, and business corporations. There should be strict limits on congressional campaign expenditures and contributions. PACs should be outlawed or severely curtailed. Public funding—direct or through discount broadcasting and postage—is needed, similar to that already provided in presidential campaigns, to level the playing field somewhat for challengers, since incumbents have an incredible advantage in fund raising, and to allow enforcement of limits on a candidate's own funds, as well as to offset the presently unrestricted independent expenditures by supposedly unconnected groups for and against congressional candidates.

Conflict in Congress.   Congress as an institution is especially, and almost always, unpopular, and the situation is not improved when members of Congress themselves run against the very body they want to be, or stay, a member of, as so many do.

Maybe there is no way to improve permanently the standing of Congress. Its own popularity suffered because of the rise in recent times of a cynicism toward government in general. Its standing has been hurt, too, by the complexity and seeming intractability of so many current issues, especially because Americans expect Congress to solve the nation's problems.

But it is the very nature of Congress that is the root cause of its major public image predicament. Like democracy itself, of which it is a part, Congress is slow, complex, and poorly reported on, as well as highly conflictual. This latter attribute is especially troublesome in regard to the popularity of Congress.

Americans like democracy, but they hate conflict. Yet conflict, and resolving it, is the essence of democracy and of the work of a legislative body, especially. Congress has become even more conflictual in recent times as it has become more open and democratic, as well as more individualistic, with the reforms and other changes wrought, particularly in the 1970s and afterward, as a result of earlier and great changes in the external environment of Congress. Congress has also become more partisan.

But all these internal reforms and changes were, for the most part, important advances, and they have helped to make Congress more like the responsive and representative body it should be and in some ways more responsible, as well. It is true, though, that Congress has, in the process, become less efficient in lawmaking.

Congress is a conflictual place because that is the way it was, and is, structured, with fragmented powers placed in opposition to each other. Conflict is especially inherent in the relationship between the Congress and the president, a veritable invitation to struggle. The Constitution makes it so by sharing out authority—such as that over appointments and treaty making—between the two branches.

Congress and the president have different, and conflict-causing, time perspectives. This difference is not just because of the different lengths of their various terms of office, but it results particularly from the fact that, since the president can only be reelected once, while the terms of senators and representatives are unlimited, and since presidential success with Congress is usually strongest at the beginning of a president's term, presidents are inevitably in a hurry, while the pace of Congress is nearly always less rushed. This difference is a part of the invitation to conflict.

So is our party system. Among other things, our system makes it possible, and since the mid-1950s, it seems, with increased split-ticket voting, almost probable, that the United States will have divided government at the national level—a president of one party and one or both houses of Congress under the control of the other. Divided government has often produced gridlock.

Congress has become a more partisan place. This change occurred primarily because, with an ideological realignment between Republican and Democratic identifiers, fueled especially by changes in the South and most notably among the party activists, the "nominators," in a sense, the party identifiers and nominators of each party, have become more internally homogeneous and more unlike those of the other party. And that, in turn, has helped to produce Senate and House parties that, likewise, are more internally homogeneous and more unlike each other—the Republicans becoming more conservative, the Democrats more moderate to liberal. Party conferences have become stronger and more assertive, the party leaders, more aggressive and, especially in the House, more powerful. Greater partisanship has produced more party responsibility and, simultaneously, greater opportunity for conflict and thus less efficiency.

The filibuster and related obstructionism.   In the U.S. Senate, where it requires sixty votes to cut off debate and allow the majority to vote, these practices have been the greatest causes of congressional gridlock in recent years, especially when there has been divided government. There was a time, during most of the Senate's history, when the norms of that body constrained members not to use their full powers or to push them to the limit. The norms of the Senate changed, but the rules that permit obstructionism did not. The filibuster and related obstructionism are particularly effective when, as now, there is a very narrow margin between the numbers of the majority party and the minority party in the Senate, and the minority (Republican) party wields a party-line filibuster, which has become common.

Party-line or not, the filibuster has been trivialized in recent times, used to block Senate action on issues that are much less than major in anybody's scheme of things. Prefilibusters—on a motion just to proceed to consideration of a measure—have become quite frequent. And, since the filibuster rule requires that consideration of a bill and voting on it must usually be accomplished by a unanimous consent agreement, worked out by the Majority Leader, one senator, alone, has come to be allowed to place a hold on legislation, to prevent it from being taken up at all.

The Senate's ability to act in an orderly and timely way is also greatly hampered by its rules and procedures. They allow nongermane amendments to be offered to nonbudget measures. They also permit the Senate to jump around from one provision of a bill to another, and back again, with no finality to a vote, since section-by-section consideration of legislation is not required.

These problems ought to be overcome to make the Senate more responsible, more able to do its work. The hold ought to be abolished, and debate on a motion to proceed should be limited to two hours. One further idea that ought to be adopted is that of activating a Senate "committee of the whole," in which debate would be limited, amendments would be required to be germane, and bills would be compelled to be considered section by section. It would be good, too, if the Senate could be persuaded to provide for a graduated reduction in the number of votes needed for cloture—sixty on the first cloture vote, fifty-five on the second, and a mere majority on the third.

The committee system.   All these reforms would go a long way toward revitalizing the Senate's lawmaking function. For both houses, so would committee reform. There are too many House and Senate committees and subcommittees, and an inflation in the membership numbers of each, particularly on the more sought-after committees, has occurred. Senators and House members have too many assignments and are literally overcommitted.

Committee and subcommittee numbers should be reduced in both houses, at least as much as the Joint Committee on the Organization of Congress has recommended. These recommendations would cut out some three dozen Senate subcommittees and limit most senators to serving on a maximum of eight committees and subcommittees, compared to the usual dozen or more now. On the House side, they would also reduce the number of subcommittees and restrict each member to two committee and four subcommittees.[3] Committees should be realigned to cover today's changed issue fields and to even out their workloads and attractiveness to members.

Really, though, the committee system in both houses needs a major overhaul, including the elimination of the present distinction between the authorization and appropriation functions, thus cutting out one level in the budget process, as a heavy majority of members of Congress who responded to a questionnaire from the Joint Committee on the Organization of Congress said they wanted done, and combining the two functions in each subject jurisdiction field in one committee. And the Senate could start by abolishing its select committees, as the House has done, except for the ethics and intelligence panels.

The budget system. The present budget system is in a mess, except that laws and rules have been adopted that limit debate on the overall budget reconciliation resolution and require that amendments offered to it be germane, all certainly to the good. The budget battles have become so partisan and start so early each session, now, that Congress should institutionalize the budget summit device, used during the Reagan administration in 1987 and the Bush administration in 1990. This device would allow a bridging over of the chasms that exist in our system, between the executive and legislative branches, between the House and the Senate, and between the political parties.

The institutionalized summit should be accompanied by the formal adoption of two-year budgeting, as the Joint Committee on the Organization of Congress has recommended, similar to multiple-year budgeting accomplished on an ad hoc basis by the last Bush budget and the first one of the Clinton administration. This reform would regularly permit a concentration in the first year of a Congress on budget matters and, in the second year, on lawmaking and oversight. A realignment of committees, again, could also effect a great improvement in the budget process and thus in the efficiency of Congress.

The United States' founders designed Congress as the people's branch of our national government, to embody, as Barbara Hinckley wrote, "the eighteenth century notion of a representative assembly and the nineteenth century innovation of a popular democracy," and, as Hinckley said further, "Congress is doing pretty much what it was designed to do."[4]

8has remained an extraordinarily stable and highly autonomous institution, which cannot be said for the legislatures of many other industrial nations, according to Samuel Patterson, who added:

If Henry Clay were alive today, and he were to serve again in the House and Senate to which he was chosen so many times in the 19th century, he would find much that was very familiar. He would certainly recognize where he was, and perhaps after some initial shock he surely would be reasonably comfortable in the modern congressional envelope.[5]

Congress is still a responsive and representative institution, more so than at some times in the past, and its members could be made even more accountable. Congress is still the national lawmaking body, and its decision making could be facilitated and made more responsible and efficient.

But, withal, Congress remains what Edward Schneier and Bertram Gross call a "true legislature," which is "in essence a nonhierarchic, territorially decentralized, autonomous, collegial, and representative institution. It is a body of generalists whose members, in a fundamental sense, are equals. And it embodies in its ideal form, such basic democratic values as liberty, equality, and popular sovereignty."[6]

The U.S. Congress is today, perhaps more than ever, a place of largely well-motivated, well-prepared, and high-minded professional members, the world's greatest deliberative body, and, as Aaron Burr said of the U.S. Senate, the citadel of America's democracy.

The defense rests.

Notes

PROLOGUE

1. See, for example, an exit poll showing 76 percent disapproval of congressional performance, cited in R. W. Apple, Jr., "Crystal Unclear: Will Tuesday's Disaffection Become Rejection at the 1992 Polls?" *New York Times* (November 11, 1990), Sec. 4, p. 1.

2. Quoted in Walter L. Updegrave, "What Congress Really Costs You: $2.8 Billion a Year," *Money* (August 1992), p. 129.

3. Quoted in Steven V. Roberts, "Oklahoma Senator's Woes Reflect G.O.P. Concerns," *New York Times* (January 5, 1986), p. A8.

4. Quoted in Alan R. Gitelson, Robert L. Dudley, and Melvin J. Dubnick, *American Government,* 3rd ed. (Boston: Houghton Mifflin, 1993), p. 261.

5. Woodrow Wilson, *Congressional Government* (New York: Meridian Books, 1956), p. 31.

6. James MacGregor Burns, *Congress on Trial: The Legislative Process and the Administrative State* (New York: Gordian Press, 1966; first published in 1949 by Harper & Brothers), p. 121.

7. Thomas E. Cronin, "The Imperial Presidency Re-examined," in William S. Livingston, Lawrence C. Dodd, and Richard L. Schott, eds., *The Presidency and the Congress* (Austin: University of Texas Press, 1979), pp. 36–37.

8. Bertram Gross and Edward V. Schneier, *Congress Today* (New York: St. Martin's Press, 1993), pp. 42, 43.

9. James MacGregor Burns, *Congress on Trial: The Legislative Process and the Administrative State*, pp. 120, 207.

10. Joseph S. Clark, *Congress: The Sapless Branch* (New York: Harper & Row, 1964), p. 23.

11. See Tom Wicker, "In the Nation: An Alienated Public," *New York Times* (November 13, 1991), p. E15.

12. *Congressional Record* (September 10, 1987), pp. S11918, S11919.

13. See E. J. Dionne, Jr., *Why Americans Hate Politics* (New York: Simon and Schuster, 1991); Seymour Martin Lipset and William Schneider, *The Confidence Gap: Business, Labor, and Government in the Public Mind*, rev. ed. (Baltimore: Johns Hopkins University Press, 1987), pp. 41–66; and Herbert B. Asher, *Presidential Elections and American Politics*, rev. ed. (Homewood, Ill.: Dorsey, 1980), p. 9.

14. Jack Dennis, "Public Support for Congress," *Political Behavior* 3 (1981), pp. 319–350.

15. Glenn R. Parker, *Characteristics of Congress* (Englewood Cliffs, N.J.: Prentice-Hall, 1989), p. 50.

16. Concerning the causes of fluctuations in congressional popularity, see Samuel C. Patterson and Gregory A. Caldeira, "Standing Up for Congress: Variations in Public Esteem Since the 1960s," *Legislative Studies Quarterly*, 15(1) (1990), pp. 25–47; Glenn R. Parker, "Some Themes in Congressional Unpopularity," *American Journal of Political Science* 21 (1977), pp. 93–109; Glenn R. Parker, *Characteristics of Congress*; and Randall B. Ripley, *Congress: Process and Policy*, 4th ed. (New York: W. W. Norton, 1988), pp. 366–368.

17. Samuel C. Patterson and Gregory A. Caldeira, "Standing Up for Congress: Variations in Public Esteem Since the 1960s," p. 40.

18. Ibid., p. 39.

19. NBC's "Meet the Press," March 14, 1993.

20. Samuel C. Patterson and Gregory A. Caldeira, "Standing Up for Congress: Variations in Public Esteem Since the 1960s," p. 36.

21. Gallup Poll News Service 55, no. 24 (October 31, 1990), p. 1.

22. Nelson W. Polsby, "Congress-Bashing for Beginners," *Public Interest* 100 (1990), pp. 15–23.

23. Reported in David J. Vogler, *The Politics of Congress,* 6th ed. (Madison, Wis.: Brown and Benchmark, 1993), pp. 16, 17.

24. *New York Times*/CBS News Poll (October 26–31, 1990), reported in *New York Times* (April 21, 1991), p. E6.

25. Reported in Marjorie Randon Hershey, "The Congressional Elections," in Gerald M. Pomper, ed., *The Election of 1992* (Chatham, N.J.: Chatham House, 1993), p. 164.

26. David J. Vogler, *The Politics of Congress*, p. 17.

27. Lawrence C. Dodd and Bruce I. Oppenheimer, "Perspectives on the 1992 Congressional Elections," in Lawrence C. Dodd and Bruce I. Oppenheimer, eds., *Congress Reconsidered*, 5th ed. (Washington, D.C.: Congressional Quarterly, 1993), p. 5.

28. Russell Baker, "Polls and Quacks: Who Elects Congress Anyway?" *New York Times* (November 5, 1991), p. A25.

CHAPTER ONE

1. Michael Tackett and Mitchell Locin, "Capitol Offense," *Chicago Tribune* (April 4, 1992), pp. 1, 4.

2. Walter L. Updegrave, "What Congress Really Costs You: $2.8 Billion a Year," *Money* (August 1992), p. 129.

3. ABC News "Nightline," Show 2,916, with Forrest Sawyer, July 27, 1992.

4. James K. Glassman, "Observer: Hysterical, Biased Account by 'Money' of Hill's Finances," *Roll Call* (July 30, 1992), p. 5.

5. Ibid.

6. Anne Willette, "Cover Story: Lawmakers' Pay, Perks Add to Total," *USA Today* (September 28, 1992), p. 1a.

7. James K. Glassman, "Observer: Hysterical, Biased Account by 'Money' of Hill's Finances," p. 24.

8. Interview, ABC News "Nightline," July 27, 1992.

9. Interview, ABC News "Nightline," July 27, 1992.

10. James K. Glassman, "Observer: Hysterical, Biased Account by 'Money' of Hill's Finances," pp. 5, 24.

11. Interview, ABC News "Nightline," July 27, 1992.

12. Material in the section is taken from Fred R. Harris, *Deadlock or Decision: The U.S. Senate and the Rise of National Politics* (New York: Oxford University Press, 1993), pp. 33–40.

13. Democratic Study Group, U.S. House of Representatives, Special Report No. 100-32, "Is It Out of Control? The Cost of Congress," (May 17, 1988), p. 1.

14. Norman J. Ornstein, Thomas E. Mann, and Michael J. Malbin, *Vital Statistics on Congress 1991–1992* (Washington, D.C.: Congressional Quarterly, 1992), p. 122.

15. Quoted in Beth Donovan, "Appropriations: Legislative Funding Total Is Less Than Last Year," *Congressional Quarterly Weekly Report* (October 10, 1992), p. 3129.

16. See Beth Donovan, "Congress Avoids Battles Over Its Funding," *Congressional Quarterly Weekly Report* (August 7, 1993), p. 2143.

17. See Jack Fincher, "What We Pay Congress (and How It Got to Be So Much)," *Constitution* (Winter 1992), pp. 45–48.

18. Quoted in Jack Fincher, "What We Pay Congress (and How It Got to Be So Much)," p. 46.

19. Mike Mills, "Raising Members' Pay: A 200-year Dilemma," *Congressional Quarterly Weekly Report* (February 4, 1989), pp. 209–212. For a general history of the congressional salary question, see Congressional Quarterly, *Congressional Pay and Perquisites: History, Facts, and Controversy* (Washington, D.C.: Congressional Quarterly, 1992).

20. See Robert S. Miller and Donald O. Dewey, "The Congressional Salary Amendment: 200 Years Later," *Glendale Law Review* (1991), 10 (1–2), p. 94.

21. Quoted in Jack Fincher, "What We Pay Congress (and How It Got to Be So Much)," p. 46.

22. James Madison, speech in the U.S. House of Representatives in support of proposed constitutional amendment, June 8, 1789, *Annals of Congress* (1789), 1 pp. 423, 440.

23. Quoted in Robert S. Miller and Donald O. Dewey, "The Congressional Salary Amendment: 200 Years Later," p. 98.

24. Jack Fincher, "What We Pay Congress (and How It Got to Be So Much)," p. 48.

25. Ibid.

26. Concerning this pay-raise fight, see Janet Hook, "Proposal for 51 Percent Pay Hike Sets Up Fracas," *Congressional Quarterly Weekly Report* (December 17, 1988), pp. 3522–3524; Janet Hook, "Congress Wavering on 51 Percent Salary Hike," *Congressional Quarterly Weekly Report* (February 4, 1989), pp. 203–208; Janet Hook, "Pay Raise Killed, but the Headaches Persist," *Congressional Quarterly Weekly Report* (February 11, 1989), pp. 261–263; Janet Hook, "How the Pay-Raise Strategy Came Unraveled," *Congressional Quarterly Weekly Report* (February 11, 1989), pp. 264–267; and Michael Oreskes, "Defeat of Congressional Pay Raise Demolishes No-Vote System," *New York Times* (February 9, 1989), p. 8.

27. For the history of the congressional salary amendment, see "Madison Amendment Surprises Lawmakers," *Congressional Quarterly Almanac 1992* (Washington, D.C.: Congressional Quarterly, 1993), pp. 58, 59; Jack Fincher, "What We Pay Congress (and How It Got to Be So Much)" and Robert S. Miller and Donald O. Dewey, "The Congressional Salary Amendment: 200 Years Later."

28. *Coleman v. Miller,* 307 U.S. 433 (1939).

29. See Jill Zuckman, "Labor: Another Partisan Gap Exposed in Jobless Benefits Bill," *Congressional Quarterly Weekly Report* (March 6, 1993), p. 519.

30. "Madison Amendment Surprises Lawmakers," *Congressional Quarterly Almanac 1992,* p. 59.

31. Bernd Debusmann, "International Comparison Shows High Cost of U.S. Democracy," Reuters report, May 20, 1992.

32. Material in this section on the British House of Commons and its relationship with the government is taken from Jorgen S. Rasmussen, *The British Political System: Concentrated Power Versus Accountability* (Belmont, Calif.: Wadsworth, 1993), pp. 93–123.

33. Ibid., p. 108.

34. On the matter of member practice of law, see Congressional Quarterly, *Congressional Ethics: History, Facts, and Controversy* (Washington, D.C.: Congressional Quarterly, 1992), pp. 152, 153.

35. On this subject, see generally Dan Clawson, Alan Neustadt, and Denise Scott, *Money Talks: Corporate PACs and Political Influence* (New York: Basic Books, 1992), pp. 76–78; and Philip M. Stern, *The Best Congress Money Can Buy* (New York: Pantheon Books, 1988), pp. 143–148.

36. Cokie Roberts, "Good Old-Fashioned Public Servants," *Washington Post* (October 28, 1992), p. A25.

37. Nelson W. Polsby, "Congress-Bashing for Beginners," *Public Interest* (1990), 100, pp. 21, 22.

38. Ibid., pp. 20–22.

39. Edward V. Schneier and Bertram Gross, *Congress Today* (New York: St. Martin's Press, 1993), p. 141.

40. Quotations are from Jack Fincher, "What We Pay Congress (and How It Got to Be So Much)," p. 47.

41. Nelson W. Polsby, "Congress-Bashing for Beginners," p. 15.

42. This and other quotes and material in this paragraph are taken from Fred R. Harris, *Deadlock or Decision: The U.S. Senate and the Rise of National Politics*, p. 85.

43. Ibid.

44. James K. Glassman, "Observer: Hysterical, Biased Account of 'Money' of Hill's Finances," p. 24.

45. Nelson W. Polsby, "Congress-Bashing for Beginners," p. 22.

46. Quoted in "Perspectives: Overheard," *Newsweek* (July 12, 1993), p. 15.

47. Nelson W. Polsby, "Congress-Bashing for Beginners," p. 20, 21.

48. Edward V. Schneier and Bertram Gross, *Congress Today,* p. 140.

49. Nelson W. Polsby, "Congress-Bashing for Beginners," p. 22.

50. Reported in Associated Press, "Heads of Most Top Colleges Earn Above $155,000 a Year," *New York Times* (May 5, 1993), p. B10.

51. James H. Rubin, Associated Press, "Most College Presidents Earn More Than $155,000," *Albuquerque Journal* (May 3, 1993), p. A4.

52. Nancy Tipton, "Job Candidates at UNM Drive Hard Bargains," *Albuquerque Journal* (July 6, 1993), pp. 1, 4.

53. Bob Hagan, "PNM Hires Ex-Admiral as New President, CEO," *Albuquerque Journal* (July 7, 1993), p. 1.

54. Quoted in Michael Tackett, "Storm Over Perks and Privilege Terrifies Congress," *Chicago Tribune* (April 1, 1992), p. 8.

55. Congressional Quarterly, *Congressional Pay and Perquisites: History, Facts, and Controversy*, p. 59.

56. Ibid.

57. See Congressional Quarterly, *Congressional Ethics: History, Facts, and Controversy*, pp. 97, 161.

58. See Michael Wines, "In Senate Streamlining Plan, Powerful Would Be Less So," *New York Times* (November 5, 1993), p. A9.

59. See Phil Kuntz, "Senate Panel Delays Report on Revising Case Review," *Congressional Quarterly Weekly Report* (August 7, 1993), p. 2145; Karen Ball, Associated Press, "Extend Laws to Cover Congress, Foley Says," *Albuquerque Journal* (August 14, 1993), p. A3; and "Issue: Congressional Reform," *Congressional Quarterly Weekly Report* (December 11, 1993), p. 3357.

60. Nelson W. Polsby, "Congress-Bashing for Beginners," p. 23.

61. Norman J. Ornstein, "Perks and Smirks: Is a Reasonable Review Possible?" *Roll Call* (March 23, 1992), p. 5.

62. Quoted in Kenneth J. Cooper and Helen Dewar, "Congress Cuts Perks: Gym Fees, Health Care, Gift Shops Affected," *Washington Post* (April 4, 1992), p. A1.

63. Ibid.

64. Norman J. Ornstein, "Perks and Smirks: Is a Reasonable Review Possible?" p. 16.

65. Ibid.

66. See "Rubbergate Scandal" in Congressional Quarterly, *Congressional Ethics: History, Facts, and Controversy*, p. 160; and Congressional Quarterly, "Additional Benefits: Congressional Privilege," *Congressional Pay and Perquisites: History, Facts, and Controversy*, p. 55.

67. Karen Foerstel, "Senate Private Dining Room Closes Its Doors," *Roll Call* (March 30, 1992), p. 18.

68. Kenneth J. Cooper and Helen Dewar, "Congress Cuts Perks: Gym Fees, Health Care, Gift Shops Affected," p. A8.

69. Norman J. Ornstein, "Perks and Smirks: Is a Reasonable Review Possible?" p. 16.

70. Concerning the House "bank" and its scandal, generally, see Congressional Quarterly, "History of the House Bank," *Congressional Quarterly Almanac 1992*, pp. 43–46; and Phil Kuntz, "Bank Probe Now a Criminal Matter; About 20 Remain Uncleared," *Congressional Quarterly Weekly Report* (December 19, 1992), p. 3879.

71. Congressional Quarterly, *Congressional Ethics: History, Facts, and Controversy*, p. 160.

72. Stuart Taylor, Jr., "Those Checks Didn't Really Bounce," *Legal Times* (1992), 14, pp. 19, 22.

73. Interview with pollster Paul Harstad, Garinhart Strategic Research, November 6, 1992.

74. Stuart Taylor, Jr., "Those Checks Didn't Really Bounce," p. 23.

75. Phil Kuntz, "Bank Probe Now a Criminal Matter: About 20 Remain Uncleared," p. 3877.

76. See Phil Kuntz, "Former Sergeant at Arms Guilty of Embezzlement," *Congressional Quarterly Weekly Report* (October 9, 1993), p. 2719.

77. This and other information for this section is taken from Congressional Quarterly, "Congressional Staff: A Member's Right Arm," *Congressional Pay and Perquisites: History, Facts, and Controversy*, pp. 65–89.

78. Ibid., p. 67.

79. Quoted in George B. Calloway, *Congress at the Crossroads* (New York: Thomas Y. Crowell, 1946), p. 157.

80. Quoted in Congressional Quarterly, *Congressional Pay and Perquisites: History, Facts, and Controversy*, p. 72.

81. Congressional Management Project, Burdette A. Loomis, Director, *Setting*

Course: A Congressional Management Guide (Washington, D.C.: American University, 1984), p. 151.

82. David J. Vogler, *The Politics of Congress* (Madison, Wis.: Brown and Benchmark, 1993), p. 76.

83. Hedrick Smith, *The Power Game: How Washington Works* (New York: Random House, 1988), p. 282.

84. Interview, ABC News "Nightline," July 27, 1992.

85. The figures are for 1991. Norman J. Ornstein, Thomas E. Mann, and Michael J. Malbin, *Vital Statistics on Congress 1993–1994* (Washington, D.C., Congressional Quarterly Press), pp. 126, 127.

86. James K. Glassman, "Observer: Hysterical, Biased Account by 'Money' of Hill's Finances," p. 24.

87. Interview, ABC News "Nightline," July 27, 1992.

88. Special Report of the Democratic Study Group of the U.S. House of Representatives, No. 100-32, "Is It Out of Control? The Cost of Congress," (May 17, 1988), p. 9.

89. See Norman J. Ornstein, Thomas E. Mann, and Michael J. Malbin, *Vital Statistics on Congress 1993–1994*, pp. 126, 127.

90. Thomas Galvin, "Legislative Spending: Pressed by Clinton's Example, Leaders Promise Cutbacks," *Congressional Quarterly Weekly Report* (February 23, 1993), pp. 387–388; and Phil Kuntz, "Trimming Congress," in Special Supplement, "When the Money Goes," *Congressional Quarterly Weekly Report* (December 11, 1993), p. 108.

91. See Thomas E. Mann and Norman Ornstein, Directors, *Renewing Congress: A First Report of the Renewing Congress Project* (Washington, D.C.: American Enterprise Institute and Brookings Institution, 1992), p. 66.

92. David J. Vogler, *The Politics of Congress,* p. 38.

93. Concerning the power of congressional staff, see Michael J. Malbin, *Unelected Representatives: Congressional Staff and the Future of Representative Government* (New York: Basic Books, 1980).

94. Reported in David W. Brady, "Personnel Management in the House," in Joseph Cooper and G. Calvin MacKenzie, eds., *The House at Work* (Austin: University of Texas Press, 1981), p. 152.

95. Ross K. Baker, *House and Senate* (New York: W. W. Norton, 1989), p. 94.

96. Ibid., p. 90.

97. Quoted in Fred R. Harris, *Deadlock or Decision: The U.S. Senate and the Rise of National Politics,* p. 108.

98. Ibid., p. 159.

99. Quoted in Congressional Quarterly, *Congressional Pay and Perquisites: History, Facts, and Controversy,* p. 76.

100. Christine DeGregorio, "Professionals in the U.S. Congress: An Analysis of Working Styles," *Legislative Studies Quarterly,* (1988), XIII, p. 166.

101. Ross W. Baker, *House and Senate,* p. 94.

102. Quoted in Harrison W. Fox, Jr., and Susan Webb Hammond, *Congressional Staffs: The Invisible Force in American Lawmaking* (New York: Free Press, 1977), p. 5.

103. See Peter Woll, *Congress* (Boston: Little, Brown, 1985), p. 191.

104. Phil Kuntz, "Reform Panel Stops Listening, Starts Thinking of Change," *Congressional Quarterly Weekly Report* (July 3, 1993), p. 1716.

CHAPTER TWO

1. Information in this section is taken from Fred R. Harris, *Deadlock or Decision: The U.S. Senate and the Rise of National Politics* (New York: Oxford University Press, 1993), pp. 36–38.

2. Personal interview by the author with Floyd Riddick, Washington, D.C., August 17, 1988.

3. See John H. Fund, "Term Limitation: An Idea Whose Times Has Come," in Gerald Benjamin and Michael J. Malbin, eds., *Limiting Legislative Terms* (Washington, D.C.: Congressional Quarterly Press, 1992), pp. 225–239.

4. Dave Marash, ABC News "Nightline," Show # 2916. July 27, 1992.

5. See "Voters Embrace Congressional Term Limits," *Congressional Quarterly Almanac 1992* (Washington, D.C.: Congressional Quarterly Press, 1993), pp. 71, 72; and James L. Sundquist, *Constitutional Reform and Effective Government,* rev. ed. (Washington, D.C.: Brookings Institution, 1992), p. 182.

6. James L. Sundquist, *Constitutional Reform and Effective Government,* rev. ed., pp. 178, 179.

7. On the early history of term limits, see American Enterprise Institute, *Limiting Presidential and Congressional Terms* (Washington, D.C.: American Enterprise Institute, 1979), pp. 5–8.

8. Jonathan Elliot, ed., *Debates on the Adoption of the Federal Constitution,* Vol. 2 (New York: Burt Franklin, 1988), p. 292.

9. Paul Leicester Ford, *Essays on the Constitution of the United States* [1892] (New York: Burt Franklin, 1970), p. 234.

10. Quoted in Mark P. Petracca, "Rotation in Office: The History of an Idea," in Gerald Benjamin and Michael J. Malbin, eds., *Limiting Legislative Terms,* p. 30.

11. Paul Leicester Ford, *Essays on the Constitution of the United States,* p. 234.

12. Jonathan Elliot, ed., *Debates on the Adoption of the Federal Constitution,* Vol. 1, (New York: Burt Frankin, 1988), pp. 292, 293.

13. Paul Leicester Ford, *Essays on the Constitution of the United States,* p. 234.

14. "Foley Joins in Effort Against Term Limits," *Congressional Quarterly Weekly Report* (June 12, 1993), p. 1504.

15. See, for example, *Storer v. Brown,* 415 U.S. 726 (1974).

16. See "Voters Embrace Congressional Term Limits," *Congressional Quarterly Almanac 1992*, p. 71.

17. 415 U.S. 726 (1969).

18. 17 *Annals of Congress* 871 (1807), quoted in *Powell v. McCormack*, 395 U.S. 486 (1969), p. 542.

19. Ibid., *Annals* 872, *Powell v. McCormack*, p. 543.

20. Joseph Story, *A Familiar Exposition of the Constitution of the United States* [1840] (New York: Harper and Brothers, 1893), quoted in Steven R. Ross and Charles Tiefer, "Brief of the *Amicus Curiae* United States Representative Lawrence J. Smith," in Gerald Benjamin and Michael J. Malbin, eds., *Limiting Legislative Terms*, p. 256.

21. An Arkansas circuit court in 1993 ruled in *Hill v. Tucker* that the state's term limits for members of Congress violated the U.S. Constitution because they attempted to add a new qualification for congressional membership, and this case may be the first on the question to go to the U.S. Supreme Court. See Jennifer S. Thompson, "Judge in Arkansas Declares Measure Unconstitutional," *Congressional Quarterly Weekly Report* (August 7, 1993), p. 2181.

22. Marjorie Randon Hershey, "The Congressional Elections," in Gerald M. Pomper, ed., *The Election of 1992* (Chatham, N.J.: Chatham House, 1992), pp. 166, 177.

23. Ibid., p. 174.

24. Rhodes Cook, "Incumbency Proves Liability in '92," *Congressional Quarterly Weekly Report* (September 12, 1992), p. 2774.

25. Norman J. Ornstein, Thomas E. Mann, and Michael J. Malbin, *Vital Statistics on Congress 1993–1994* (Washington, D.C.: Congressional Quarterly Press, 1992), pp. 19, 20.

26. Quoted in John Fund, "Term Limitation: An Idea Whose Time Has Come," p. 232.

27. Marjorie Randon Hershey, "The Congressional Elections," pp. 184, 185.

28. John R. Hibbing, "Careerism in Congress: For Better or for Worse?" in Lawrence C. Dodd and Bruce I. Oppenheimer, eds., *Congress Reconsidered*, 5th ed. (Washington, D.C.: Congressional Quarterly Press, 1993), pp. 67, 68.

29. James L. Sundquist, *Constitutional Reform and Effective Government*, rev. ed., pp. 184, 185.

30. Ibid., p. 183.

31. R. Douglas Arnold, "Can Inattentive Citizens Control Their Elected Representatives?" in Lawrence C. Dodd and Bruce I. Oppenheimer, eds., *Congress Reconsidered*, 5th ed., pp. 407, 408.

32. This statement was made concerning state legislatures and term limits that might encourage "musical chairs." Michael J. Malbin and Gerald Benjamin, "Legislatures After Term Limits," in Gerald Benjamin and Michael J. Malbin, eds., *Limiting Legislative Terms*, p. 211.

33. On this point, see Fred R. Harris, *Deadlock or Decision: The U.S. Senate and the Rise of National Politics* (New York: Oxford University Press, 1993), p. 97.

34. Ibid.

35. Quoted in Charles R. Kesler, "Bad Housekeeping: The Case Against Congressional Term Limits," in Gerald Benjamin and Michael J. Malbin, eds., *Limiting Legislative Terms*, p. 248.

36. Linda L. Fowler, "A Comment on Competition and Careers," in Gerald Benjamin and Michael J. Malbin, eds., *Limiting Legislative Terms*, p. 183.

37. Nelson W. Polsby, "Congress-Bashing for Beginners, *Public Interest* (1990), 100, pp. 20, 21.

38. Edward V. Schneier and Bertram Gross, *Congress Today* (New York: St. Martin's Press, 1993), p. 501.

39. Ibid, p. 21.

40. Quoted in Gary Copeland, "Term Limits and Political Careers in Oklahoma: In, Out, Up, or Down," in Gerald Benjamin and Michael J. Malbin, eds., *Limiting Legislative Terms*, p. 154.

41. Ibid.

42. Joel Brinkley, "A Strategy on the Budget: Go After the Greenhorns," *New York Times* (July 23, 1993), pp. A1, A7.

43. Suzanne Garment, *Scandal: The Crisis of Mistrust in American Politics* (New York: Times Books, 1991), p. 6.

44. Quoted in Helen Dewar, "A Question of Ethics," *Washington Post National Weekly Edition* (January 11–17, 1993), p. 6.

45. Suzanne Garment, *Scandal: The Crisis of Mistrust in American Politics*, p. 6.

46. See Drew Pearson and Jack Anderson, *The Case Against Congress* (New York: Simon and Schuster, 1968), p. 204; and *Congressional Quarterly Almanac 1962* (Washington, D.C.: Congressional Quarterly Press, 1962), p. 992.

47. For their recommendations, see Drew Pearson and Jack Anderson, *The Case Against Congress*, pp. 451, 452.

48. Quoted in Helen Dewar, "A Question of Ethics," *Washington Post National Weekly Edition*, p. 7.

49. Personal interview by the author, Washington, D.C., September 15, 1988.

50. Larry J. Sabato, *Feeding Frenzy: How Attack Journalism Has Transformed American Politics* (New York: Free Press, 1991).

51. See Marianna A. Levinas, "Committee Urged to Tighten Rules on Accepting Gifts," *Congressional Quarterly Weekly Report* (July 24, 1993), p. 1931; and "House on Defensive Over Gift Rules," *Congressional Quarterly Weekly Report* (October 2, 1993), p. 2616.

52. See Beth Donovan, "Senate Passes Bill to Tighten Special Interest Disclosure," *Congressional Quarterly Weekly Report* (May 8, 1993), pp. 1123, 1124.

53. Nelson W. Polsby, "Congress-Bashing for Beginners," p. 23.

54. Edward V. Schneier and Bertram Gross, *Congress Today*, pp. 496, 497.

55. Nelson W. Polsby, "The Institutionalization of the U.S. House of Representatives," *American Political Science Review* (1968), 62, pp. 144–168.

56. Information in this paragraph is taken from John R. Alford and David W. Brady, "Personal and Partisan Advantage in U.S. Congressional Elections, 1846–1990," in Lawrence C. Dodd and Bruce I. Oppenheimer, eds., *Congress Reconsidered*, 5th ed., pp. 141–157.

57. See James L. Sundquist, *Constitutional Reform and Effective Government*, rev. ed., p. 185.

58. Melissa Collie and Gary Jacobson, cited in John R. Alford and David W. Brady, "Personal and Partisan Advantage in U.S. Congressional Elections, 1846–1990," p. 154.

59. Ibid., 155; and Marjorie Randon Hershey, "The Congressional Elections," pp. 160–166.

60. Edward V. Schneier and Bertram Gross, *Congress Today*, pp. 93, 94.

61. John R. Hibbing, "Careerism in Congress: For Better or for Worse?" p. 72.

62. On this point, see Fred R. Harris, *Deadlock or Decision: The U.S. Senate and the Rise of National Politics*, pp. 57–59; and Robert S. Erikson and Gerald C. Wright, "Voters, Candidates, and Issues in Congressional Elections," in Lawrence C. Dodd and Bruce I. Oppenheimer, eds., *Congress Reconsidered*, 5th ed., pp. 110, 111.

63. Robert S. Erikson and Gerald C. Wright, "Voters, Candidates, and Issues in Congressional Elections," p. 103.

64. Thomas E. Mann, *Unsafe at Any Margin: Interpreting Congressional Elections* (Washington, D.C.: American Enterprise Institute, 1978), pp. 23, 24.

65. Quoted in "Candidates and Process Wounded in 'Total War,'" *New York Times* (March 19, 1990), p. A14.

66. John R. Hibbing, "Careerism in Congress: For Better or for Worse?" p. 78.

67. Ibid., p. 76.

68. Robert S. Erikson and Gerald C. Wright, "Voters, Candidates, and Issues in Congressional Elections," p. 108.

69. John R. Hibbing, "Careerism in Congress: For Better or for Worse?" p. 80.

70. John R. Alford and David W. Brady, "Personal and Partisan Advantage in U.S. Congressional Elections, 1846–1990," p. 151.

71. Edward M. Schneier and Bertram Gross, *Congress Today*, p. 80.

72. James R. Alford and David W. Brady, "Personal and Partisan Advantage in Congressional Elections, 1846–1990," p. 153.

73. Martin P. Wattenberg, *The Decline of American Political Parties 1952–1988* (Cambridge, Mass.: Harvard University Press, 1990), p. 165.

74. See David Mayhew, "Congressional Elections: The Case of the Vanishing Marginals," *Polity* (Spring 1974), 7, p. 311; and John R. Alford and David W. Brady, "Personal and Partisan Advantage in U.S. Congressional Elections, 1846–1990," pp. 151–154.

75. Clifford Kraus, "Political Memo: Vying for Committees, Freshmen Mimic Elders," *New York Times* (November 30, 1992), p. A9.

76. "Freshman Class: No Reform Juggernaut," *Congressional Quarterly Weekly Report* (April 24, 1993), p. 99. See also Beth Donovan, "Fractures in Freshman Class Weaken Impact on House," *Congressional Quarterly Weekly Report* (April 3, 1993), pp. 807–810.

77. See Alan I. Abramowitz, "Incumbency, Campaign Spending, and the Decline of Competition in U.S. House Elections," *Journal of Politics* (August 1991), 53, p. 35.

78. See Kenneth N. Bickers and Robert M. Stein, "Congressional Elections and the Pork Barrel," paper delivered at the annual meeting of the American Political Science Association, Chicago, September 1992.

79. Mark Bisnow, *In the Shadow of the Dome: Chronicles of a Capitol City Aide*, (New York: Morrow, 1990), quoted in Congressional Quarterly, *Congressional Ethics: History, Facts, and Controversy* (Washington, D.C.: Congressional Quarterly Press, 1992), p. 104.

80. See Harrison W. Fox, Jr., and Susan W. Hammond, *Congressional Staffs: The Invisible Force in American Lawmaking* (New York: The Free Press, 1977), p. 66.

81. Material in this paragraph is taken from Congressional Quarterly, *Congressional Ethics: History, Facts, and Controversy*, pp. 104, 105.

82. This and other information about the franking privilege, unless indicated otherwise, is taken from Congressional Quarterly, *Congressional Pay and Perquisites: History, Facts, and Controversy* (Washington, D.C.: Congressional Quarterly, 1992), pp. 27–36.

83. These and related figures concerning the franking privilege are taken from Norman J. Ornstein, Thomas E. Mann, and Michael J. Malbin, *Vital Statistics on Congress 1991–1992*, pp. 122, 139, 160, 161.

84. Ibid., p. 122.

85. "House Tightens Limits on Franked Mail," *Congressional Quarterly Almanac 1992*, p. 61.

86. See Beth Donovan, "Congress Avoids Battles Over Its Own Funding," p. 2143.

87. "Highlights of Campaign Finance Bill As Passed by the Senate on June 17," *Congressional Quarterly Weekly Report* (June 19, 1993), p. 1537.

88. See Jennifer S. Thompson, "With So Many Seats Open in '92, Campaign Spending Rose 52%," *Congressional Quarterly Weekly Report* (March 20, 1993), p. 691.

89. See "Research & Readings: Congressional Candidate Spending Up 52% in '92," *Campaigns & Elections* (April/May 1993), p. 76; Beth Donovan, "'92 Numbers Suggest Big Changes If Campaign Finance Bill Passes," *Congressional Quarterly Weekly Report* (February 27, 1993), p. 693; and "FEC Reports: Senate Candidates," *Congressional Quarterly Weekly Report* (March 20, 1993), p. 692.

90. Beth Donovan, "'92 Numbers Suggest Big Changes If Campaign Finance Bill Passes," p. 437.

91. Ibid.

92. From interviews with U.S. Senators by the Center for Responsive Politics, Washington, D.C., compiled April 30, 1987, and made available to the author with the understanding that the identities of the senators would not be disclosed.

93. Quoted in Jack W. Germond and Jules Whitcover, "Inside Politics: Looking for a Smoking Gun on Campaign Funds?" *National Journal* (December 12, 1989), p. 2956.

94. Federal Election Commission report, cited in Charles R. Babcock, "Leaders of the PACs: NRA, UPS and Dentists," *Washington Post National Weekly Edition* (May 10–16, 1993), p. 13.

95. Direct-mail letter, quoted in Larry J. Sabato, *PAC Power: Inside the World of Political Action Committees* (New York: W. W. Norton, 1985), p. xi.

96. Marjorie Randon Hershey, "The Congressional Elections," p. 159.

97. Gary C. Jacobson, "The Misallocation of Resources in House Campaigns," in Lawrence C. Dodd and Bruce I. Oppenheimer, eds., *Congress Reconsidered*, 5th ed., p. 119.

98. Ibid.

99. Federal Election Commission report, cited in Charles R. Babcock, "Leaders of the PACs: NRA, UPS and Dentists," p. 13.

100. Beth Donovan and Ilyse J. Veron, "Freshman Got to Washington with Help of PAC Funds," *Congressional Quarterly Weekly Report* (March 27, 1993), p. 723.

101. Beth Donovan, "Delay, Controversy Certain as Senate Takes Up Plan," *Congressional Quarterly Weekly Report* (May 22, 1993), p. 1273.

102. Federal Election Commission report, cited in "Planning Ahead: What Senators Raised in the First Half of 1993," *New York Times* (August 13, 1993), p. A9.

103. Concerning the 1993 House campaign-finance reform bill, see Beth Donovan, "House Will Vote on Limits Nearing $1 Million in '96." *Congressional Quarterly Weekly Report* (November 13, 1993), pp. 3091–3093; and Beth Donovan, "House Takes First Big Step in Overhauling System," *Congressional Quarterly Weekly Report* (November 27, 1993), pp. 3246–3249.

104. Quoted in Kenneth J. Cooper and David S. Broder, "Campaign Reform, On the House," *Washington Post National Weekly Edition* (November 29–December 5, 1993), p. 13.

CHAPTER THREE

1. The poll conducted for the Democratic Leadership Council, as well as the comments of the pollster, Stanley B. Greenberg, are reported in Dan Balz, "The

Parties Ponder the Perot Phenomenon,'' *Washington Post National Weekly Edition* (July 19–25, 1993), p. 12; and David S. Broder, "While President Summiteers, Washington Speculates on Perot,'' *Albuquerque Journal* (July 12, 1993), p. A9.

2. Reported in David S. Broder, "While President Summiteers, Washington Speculates on Perot.''

3. CNN/*USA Today*/Gallup survey of July 19, 1993, reported in "Research and Readings: Congress Approval Down,'' *Campaigns and Elections* (September 1993), p. 51.

4. Glenn R. Parker, "Can Congress Ever Be a Popular Institution?'' in Joseph Cooper and G. Calvin Mackenzie, eds., *The House at Work* (Austin: University of Texas Press, 1981), pp. 32, 33.

5. Poll reported in Robert A. Dahl, "Americans Struggle To Cope with a New Political Order That Works in Opaque and Mysterious Ways,'' in Institute of Governmental Studies, University of California, Berkeley, *Public Affairs Report* (September 1993), p. 5.

6. See Randall B. Ripley, *Congress: Process and Policy*, 3rd ed. (New York: W. W. Norton, 1983), p. 429.

7. Surveys by the Center for Political Studies, University of Michigan, 1992, and the *Los Angeles Times*, 1993, reported in "America the Cynical,'' *Time* (July 1993), p. 17; and, for April 1993, a *Washington Post*/ABC News survey, reported in Richard Morin, "I'm OK; My Government's Not,'' *Washington Post National Weekly Edition* (July 26–August 1, 1993), p. 37.

8. Polls reported in Richard Morin, "I'm OK; My Government's Not,'' p. 37.

9. Glenn R. Parker, "Can Congress Ever Be a Popular Institution?'' p. 36.

10. Ibid., pp. 36, 37, citing 1974 and 1976 survey data from the Survey Research Center, University of Michigan.

11. Jack Citrin, "Why Can't Government Do the Right Thing?'' in Institute of Governmental Studies, University of California, Berkeley, *Public Affairs Report* (September 1993), p. 11.

12. Lawrence C. Dodd, "Congress and the Politics of Renewal: Redressing the Crisis of Legitimation,'' in Lawrence C. Dodd and Bruce I. Oppenheimer, eds., *Congress Reconsidered,* 5th ed. (Washington, D.C.: Congressional Quarterly Press, 1993), p. 422.

13. Glenn R. Parker, "Can Congress Ever Be a Popular Institution?'' p. 34.

14. See Catherine E. Rudder, "Can Congress Govern?'' in Lawrence C. Dodd and Bruce I. Oppenheimer, eds., *Congress Reconsidered,* 5th ed., p. 366.

15. Reported in Robert Pear, "Poverty in U.S. Grows Faster Than Population Last Year,'' *New York Times* (October 5, 1993), p. A10.

16. See Glenn R. Parker, "Can Congress Ever Be a Popular Institution?'' p. 39.

17. Samuel C. Patterson and Gregory A. Caldeira, "Standing Up for Congress: Variations in Public Esteem Since the 1960s,'' *Legislative Studies Quarterly* 15, no. 1 (February 1990), p. 40.

18. Ibid., p. 26.

19. Survey of press opinion by Kimberley Coursen of the American Enterprise Institute, reported in Dirksen Center, *Congress* (Spring/Summer 1993), pp. 1, 6.

20. Glenn R. Parker, "Can Congress Ever Be a Popular Institution?" pp. 49, 50.

21. Samuel C. Patterson and Gregory A. Caldeira, "Standing Up for Congress: Variations in Public Esteem Since the 1960s," p. 39.

22. Glenn R. Parker, "Can Congress Ever Be a Popular Institution?" p. 49.

23. Randall B. Ripley, *Congress: Process and Policy*, 4th ed. (New York: W. W. Norton, 1988), p. 366.

24. Glenn R. Parker, "Can Congress Ever Be a Popular Institution?" p. 49.

25. Eileen Burgin, "Congress and Foreign Policy: The Misperceptions," in Lawrence C. Dodd and Bruce I. Oppenheimer, eds., *Congress Reconsidered*, 5th ed., p. 352.

26. G. Calvin Mackenzie, "Coping in a Complex Age: Challenge, Response, and Reform in the House of Representatives," in Joseph Cooper and G. Calvin Mackenzie, eds., *The House at Work*, p. 14.

27. See Randall B. Ripley, *Power in the Senate* (New York: St. Martin's Press, 1969), pp. 6–19. Ripley developed these models for the U.S. Senate, but they are also applicable to the U.S. House of Representatives.

28. Anonymous senator quoted in David W. Rohde, Norman J. Ornstein, and Robert L. Peabody, "Political Change and Legislative Norms in the U.S. Senate, 1957–1974," in Glen R. Parker, ed., *Studies of Congress* (Washington, D.C.: Congressional Quarterly Press, 1985), p. 158.

29. Material in this section concerning the nationalization of American society, issues, interest groups, and Senate campaigns is taken from Fred R. Harris, *Deadlock or Decision: The U.S. Senate and the Rise of National Politics* (New York: Oxford University Press, 1993), pp. 33-88.

30. Larry J. Sabato, *Feeding Frenzy: How Attack Journalism Has Transformed American Politics* (New York: Free Press, 1991), pp. 25, 26.

31. Material in this section on how the Senate changed as power became more individualized is taken from Fred R. Harris, *Deadlock or Decision: The U.S. Senate and the Rise of National Politics*, pp. 91–158.

32. Norman J. Ornstein, Thomas E. Mann, and Michael J. Malbin, *Vital Statistics on Congress 1993–1994* (Washington, D.C.: American Enterprise Institute, 1993), p. 116.

33. Steven S. Smith, *Call to Order: Floor Politics in the House and Senate* (Washington, D.C.: Brookings Institution, 1989), p. 10.

34. Barbara Sinclair, "Congressional Reform," in James L. Sundquist, ed., *Beyond Gridlock? Prospects for Governance in the Clinton Years—and After* (Washington, D.C.: Brookings Institution, 1993), pp. 39, 40.

35. Glenn R. Parker, "Can Congress Ever Be a Popular Institution?" p. 39.

36. Ibid., p. 40.

37. Randall B. Ripley, *Congress: Process and Policy,* 3rd ed., p. 429.

38. Samuel C. Patterson and Gregory A. Caldeira, "Standing Up for Congress: Variations in Public Esteem Since the 1960s," p. 40.

39. Reported in Phillip S. Davis, "Politics, Drop in Senate Support Put Bush's Ratings in Cellar," *Congressional Quarterly Weekly Report* (December 19, 1992), pp. 3841–3844.

40. Roger H. Davidson and Walter J. Oleszek, *Congress and Its Members*, 4th ed. (Washington, D.C.: Congressional Quarterly Press, 1994), p. 249.

41. Reported in Mark Stencel, "Gridspeak: The Language of Immobility," *Washington Post* (August 3, 1992), p. A9.

42. Helen Dewar, "Good Riddance to the 102nd," *Washington Post National Weekly Edition* (October 19–25, 1992), p. 31.

43. See Edward S. Corwin, *The President: Office and Powers, 1787–1957*, 4th rev. ed. (New York: New York University Press, 1957), p. 171; and Fred R. Harris and Paul L. Hain, *America's Legislative Processes: Congress and the States* (Glenview, Ill.: Scott, Foresman, 1983), p. 393.

44. Richard E. Neustadt, *Presidential Power* (New York: Wiley, 1960), p. 33.

45. Reported in George J. Schulz, ed., *Creation of the Senate: From the Proceedings of the Federal Convention, Philadelphia, May–September, 1787*, U.S. Senate Bicentennial Publication No. 3 (Washington, D.C.: U.S. Government Printing Office, 1987), pp. 8, 11, 36, 37, 40.

46. Roy Swanstrom, *The United States Senate 1787–1801*, Senate Document 99-19 (Washington, D.C.: U.S. Government Printing Office, 1985), pp. 115–120.

47. Quoted in Richard Allen Baker, *The Senate of the United States: A Bicentennial History* (Malabar, Fla.: Robert E. Krieger Publishing, 1988), p. 21.

48. Quoted in James Q. Wilson, *American Government: Institutions and Policy*, 4th ed. (Lexington, Mass.: D. C. Heath, 1989), p. 324.

49. See Roy Swanstrom, *The United States Senate 1787–1801*, pp. 95–99.

50. Material concerning the Tower confirmation fight is taken from Fred R. Harris, *Deadlock or Decision: The U.S. Senate and the Rise of National Politics*, pp. 159–63.

51. Presidential press conference, reported in *New York Times* (March 8, 1989), p. A12.

52. Quoted in Pat Towell, "Senate Panel Deals Bush His First Defeat," *Congressional Quarterly Weekly Report* (February 25, 1989), p. 396.

53. Quoted in Dan Balz, "How Tower Used His 'No' Vote," *Washington Post* (March 8, 1989), p. A21.

54. Material concerning the Thomas confirmation fight is taken from Fred R. Harris, *Deadlock or Decision: The U.S. Senate and the Rise of National Politics*, pp. 3–4, 163–164.

55. Quoted in the syndicated column of David S. Broder, "Senate's 'Advise and Consent' Role Has Fallen into the Gutter," published in *Albuquerque Journal* (October 13, 1991), p. B3.

56. Mark Silverstein, "The People, the Senate and the Court: The Democratization of the Judicial Confirmation System," *Constitutional Commentary* 9 (Winter 1992), p. 56.

57. Hiller B. Zobel, "Naming a Justice: It Has Always Been Politics as Usual," *American Heritage* 42 (October 1991), pp. 94–95, 97–101.

58. Stanley Feingold, "Sure It's Politics: When Wasn't It?" *National Law Journal* 13 (September 2, 1991), pp. 17.

59. Ibid., p. 18.

60. *Congressional Record* (October 15, 1991), p. 14634.

61. Roger H. Davidson and Walter J. Oleszek, *Congress and Its Members,* 4th ed., p. 257.

62. Norman J. Ornstein, Thomas E. Mann, and Michael J. Malbin, *Vital Statistics on Congress 1993–1994,* pp. 20, 21.

63. Concerning the decline in party loyalty, see Fred R. Harris, *Deadlock or Decision: The U.S. Senate and the Rise of National Politics,* p. 167.

64. Martin P. Wattenberg, *The Decline of American Political Parties 1952–1988* (Cambridge, Mass.: Harvard University Press, 1990), p. 165.

65. Except as otherwise indicated, information in this section is taken from James P. Pfiffner, "The President and the Postreform Congress," in Roger H. Davidson, ed., *The Postreform Congress* (New York: St. Martin's Press, 1992), pp. 226–229; and James P. Pfiffner, "Divided Government and the Problem of Governance," in James A. Thurber, ed., *Divided Democracy: Cooperation and Conflict Between the President and Congress* (Washington, D.C.: Congressional Quarterly Press, 1991), pp. 39–60.

66. Phillip A. Davis, "Politics, Drop in Senate Support Put Bush's Ratings in the Cellar," p. 3842.

67. Ibid.

68. James Sundquist, "Needed: A Political Theory for the New Era of Coalition Government in the United States," *Political Science Quarterly* 103 (Winter 1988–1989), p. 629.

69. Phil Duncan and Steve Langdon, "When Congress Had To Choose, It Voted to Back Clinton," *Congressional Quarterly Weekly Report* (December 18, 1993), pp. 3427–3431; and Marc Birtel, "Clinton Bested by Ike and LBJ," *Congressional Quarterly Weekly Report* (December 18, 1993), p. 3429.

70. Ibid.

71. Material in this section is taken from Fred R. Harris, *Deadlock or Decision: The U.S. Senate and the Rise of National Politics,* pp. 164–188.

72. William M. Lunch, *The Nationalization of American Politics* (Berkeley: University of California Press, 1987), p. 110. See also Earl Black and Merle Black, *Politics and Society in the South* (Cambridge, Mass.: Harvard University Press, 1987), pp. 312–316.

73. See Larry J. Sabato, *The Party's Just Begun: Shaping Political Parties for America's Future* (Glenview, Ill.: Scott, Foresman, 1988), p. 122.

74. See Thomas Byrne Edsall, "The Return of Inequality," *Atlantic Monthly* (June 1938), p. 93; and Larry J. Sabato, *The Party's Just Begun*, p. 123.

75. Larry J. Sabato, *The Party's Just Begun*, pp. 124, 142; and James Allan Davis and Tom W. Smith, *General Survey, 1972–1988* (Chicago: National Opinion Research Center, 1988).

76. Gerald M. Pomper, *Voters, Elections, and Parties: The Practice of Democratic Theory* (New Brunswick, N.J.: Transaction Books, 1988), p. 289.

77. See *Public Opinion* (January/February 1987), p. 34; Gerald M. Pomper, *Voters, Elections, and Parties: The Practice of Democratic Theory*, p. 389; and Thomas B. Edsall, "Introduction," in Warren E. Miller and John R. Petrocik, eds., *Where's the Party? An Assessment of Changes in Party Loyalty and Party Coalitions in the 1980s* (Washington, D.C.: Center for National Policy, 1987), pp. 7, 8.

78. William M. Lunch, *The Nationalization of American Politics*, p. 37.

79. Walter J. Stone, Ronald B. Rapoport, and Alan J. Rabinowitz, "The Reagan Revolution and Party Polarization in the 1980s," in L. Sandy Maisel, ed., *The Parties Respond: Changes in the America Party System* (Boulder, Colo.: Westview Press, 1990), pp. 67–93.

80. Keith T. Poole and Howard Rosenthal, "The Polarization of American Politics," *Journal of Politics* 46 (1984), p. 1075.

81. See David W. Rohde, *Parties and Leaders in the Postreform House* (Chicago: University of Chicago Press, 1991).

82. See Andrew Taylor, "Southern Democrats May Score If Fading Alliance Dissolves," *Congressional Quarterly Weekly Report* (December 19, 1992), pp. 3845–3848; and Bob Benenson, "Clinton Keeps Southern Wing On His Team in 1993," *Congressional Quarterly Weekly Report* (December 18, 1993), pp. 3435–3438.

83. See David W. Rohde, *Parties and Leaders in the Postreform House* (Chicago: University of Chicago Press, 1991).

84. See Holly Edelson, "Signs Point to Greater Loyalty on Both Sides of the Aisle," *Congressional Quarterly Weekly Report* (December 19, 1992), pp. 3849–3851.

85. See Kitty Cunningham, "With Democrat in the White House, Partisanship Hits New High," *Congressional Quarterly Weekly Report* (December 18, 1993), pp. 3432–3434.

86. See, for example, concerning the Senate, Steven S. Smith, "Forces of Change in Senate Party Leadership and Organization," in Lawrence C. Dodd and Bruce I. Oppenheimer, eds., *Congress Reconsidered*, 5th ed., p. 268; and, concerning key votes in both houses in 1993, see "Democratic Support for Clinton Was Hard-Won, Rarely Certain," *Congressional Quarterly Weekly Report* (December 18, 1993), pp. 3441–3459.

87. Ibid.; and Kitty Cunningham, "With Democrat in the White House, Partisanship Hits New High," pp. 3432–3434.

88. See Fred R. Harris, *Deadlock or Decision: The U.S. Senate and the Rise*

of National Politics, pp. 164–188; and Barbara Sinclair, "House Majority Leadership in an Era of Legislative Constraint," in Roger H. Davidson, ed., *The Postreform Congress*, pp. 91–93.

89. Jack Citrin, "Why Can't Government Do the Right Thing?" p. 9.

90. See Barbara Sinclair, "Congressional Reform," pp. 39, 40; and Holly Edelson, "Signs Point to Greater Loyalty on Both Sides of the Aisle," p. 3851.

91. Jack Citrin, "Why Can't Government Do the Right Thing?" p. 10.

92. American Political Science Association, *Toward a More Responsible Two-Party System*, published as a supplement to the *American Political Science Review* 44 (September 1950), p. 17.

CHAPTER FOUR

1. Catalina Camia, "Grazing Fee Filibuster Continues, Bottling Up Interior Spending," *Congressional Quarterly Weekly Report* (October 23, 1993), p. 2875.

2. Information concerning this issue is taken from Catalina Camia, "Grazing Fee Filibuster Continues, Bottling Up Interior Spending," pp. 2875–2879; Catalina Camia, "Babbitt and Western Democrats Reach Pact on Grazing Fees," *Congressional Quarterly Weekly Report* (October 9, 1993), pp. 2723–2724; and Catalina Camia, "Senate Votes to Block Increase in Grazing Fees Next Year," *Congressional Quarterly Weekly Report* (September 18, 1993), pp. 2449–2451.

3. Quoted in Mike Mills, "House Ends Weeks of Delay, Approves Interior Spending," *Congressional Quarterly Weekly Report* (July 25, 1992), p. 2170.

4. See "Issue: Grazing Fees," *Congressional Quarterly Weekly Report* (October 31, 1992), p. 3472.

5. Concerning the filibuster and other inefficient and obstructionist Senate practices, see Fred R. Harris, *Deadlock or Decision: The U.S. Senate and the Rise of National Politics* (New York: Oxford University Press, 1993), pp. 13–23, 154–158.

6. Franklin L. Burdette, *Filibustering in the Senate* (Princeton, N.J.: Princeton University Press, 1940), p. 5.

7. Ibid., pp. 121, 122.

8. Allen Drury, *Advise and Consent* (New York: Doubleday, 1959); and William S. White, *The Citadel: The Story of the U.S. Senate* (New York: Harper, 1956).

9. Donald R. Matthews, *U.S. Senators and Their World* (Chapel Hill: University of North Carolina Press, 1960).

10. Comments of Nelson W. Polsby as a panelist at the Hendricks Symposium on the U.S. Senate, University of Nebraska, Lincoln, October 6–8, 1988.

11. Barbara Sinclair, *The Transformation of the U.S. Senate* (Baltimore: Johns Hopkins University Press, 1989), p. 139.

12. Statement of Senate Majority Leader George Mitchell (D., Maine), reported by Steven Smith, "Congressional Reform," in James L. Sundquist, ed., *Beyond*

Gridlock? Prospects for Governance in the Clinton Years—and After (Washington, D.C.: Brookings Institution, 1993), p. 48.

13. Steven S. Smith, "Congressional Reform," p. 48.

14. Rogers for the *Pittsburgh Post-Gazette,* reprinted in Ann Devroy and David S. Broder, "A Funny Thing Happened on the Way to the Senate," *Washington Post National Weekly Edition* (April 19–25, 1993), p. 13.

15. Ruth Marcus and Helen Dewar, "Learning About Life in the Senate," *Washington Post National Weekly Edition* (April 12–18, 1993), p. 12.

16. Helen Dewar, "Bob Dole, Feeling His Votes," *Washington Post National Weekly Edition* (May 10–16, 1993), p. 12.

17. Concerning the hold, see Steven S. Smith, *Call to Order: Floor Politics in the House and Senate* (Washington, D.C.: Brookings Institution, 1989), pp. 110–123.

18. "In the Senate of the 1980s, Teamwork Has Given Way to the Rule of Individuals," *Congressional Quarterly Weekly Report* (September 4, 1982), pp. 2175–2182.

19. Statement made at Hearings on Changes to Senate Rules, Rules Committee, U.S. Senate, December 2, 1987.

20. See Adam Clymer, "House Members Seek Senate Change," *New York Times* (October 21, 1993), p. A13.

21. Ibid.

22. Warren B. Rudman, in Steven S. Smith, "Congressional Reform," p. 52.

23. Steven S. Smith, in "Congressional Reform," p. 47.

24. See Lawrence C. Dodd, "A Theory of Congressional Cycles: Solving the Puzzle of Change," in Gerald C. Wright, Jr., Leroy N. Rieselbach, and Lawrence C. Dodd, eds., *Congress and Policy Change* (New York: Agathon Press, 1979), pp. 3–44.

25. Steven S. Smith, "Congressional Reform," pp. 49, 51.

26. For a report on the recommendations of the Senate side of the Joint Committee on the Organization of Congress, see Janet Hook, "Senators Offer Their Changes to Committees, Procedures," *Congressional Quarterly Weekly Report* (November 6, 1993), pp. 3030–3031.

27. Steven S. Smith, "Congressional Reform," pp. 49, 50.

28. Thomas E. Mann and Norman J. Ornstein, directors, *Renewing Congress: A Second Report of the Renewing Congress Project* (Washington, D.C.: American Enterprise Institute and Brookings Institution, 1993), p. 53.

29. Woodrow Wilson, *Congressional Government* (New York: Meridian, 1956), pp. 69, 146. This book was first published by Houghton Mifflin in 1885.

30. Thomas E. Mann and Norman J. Ornstein, directors, *Renewing Congress: A Second Report of the Renewing Congress Project,* pp. 15, 16.

31. See Norman J. Ornstein, Thomas E. Mann, and Michael J. Malbin, *Vital Statistics on Congress 1993–1994* (Washington, D.C.: Congressional Quarterly, 1993), pp. 109–115.

32. Frederick H. Pauls and Judy Schneider, CRS Issue Brief, "Congressional Reform," Congressional Research Service, Library of Congress, Updated August 10, 1992, p. 3.

33. See "Committee System: The Labyrinth," *Congressional Quarterly Weekly Report* (June 6, 1992), p. 1584.

34. See Kevin Merida, "Down the Slippery Slopes of Inside Baseball," *Washington Post National Weekly Edition* (May 10–16, 1993), p. 34.

35. See Fred R. Harris, *Deadlock or Decision: The U.S. Senate and the Rise of National Politics*, p. 139; and "The New Congress," Special Report, *Congressional Quarterly Weekly Report* (January 16, 1993), pp. 150, 151.

36. Thomas E. Mann and Norman Ornstein, directors, *Renewing Congress: A Second Report of the Renewing Congress Project*, p. 19.

37. Ibid., p. 18.

38. See Norman J. Ornstein, Thomas E. Mann, and Michael J. Malbin, *Vital Statistics on Congress 1993–1994*, p. 116.

39. Information in this section is taken from "Players, Politics and Turf of the 103rd Congress," Committee Guide Supplement, *Congressional Quarterly Weekly Report* (May 1, 1993), pp. 48–97.

40. Ibid., pp. 10–46.

41. Ibid., pp. 10–97.

42. Frederick H. Pauls and Judy Schneider, CRS Issue Brief, "Congressional Reform," p. 3.

43. Thomas E. Mann and Norman J. Ornstein, directors, *Renewing Congress: A Second Report of the Renewing Congress Project*, p. 17.

44. Peter Woll, *Congress* (Boston: Little, Brown, 1985), p. 313.

45. Quoted in "The Senate Is Not in Order," *Washington Post* (January 27, 1988).

46. Quoted in Kevin Merida, "Down the Slippery Slopes of Inside Baseball," p. 34.

47. Statement before the U.S. Senate Committee on Rules and Administration, February 25, 1988.

48. Thomas E. Mann and Norman Ornstein, directors, *Renewing Congress: A Second Report of the Renewing Congress Project*, p. 17.

49. See Phil Kuntz, "Reform Panel Stops Listening, Starts Thinking of Change," *Congressional Quarterly Weekly Report* (July 3, 1993), p. 1716.

50. Statement of U.S. Senator Nancy Kassebaum (R., Kan.) before the U.S. Senate Committee on Rules and Administration, February 25, 1988; S. Res. 260, U.S. Senate, 100th Congress, June 1987; and Senate Committee on Rules and Administration, Report on Senate Operations 1988, 100th Congress, 2nd Session, September 20, 1988, pp. 45–49.

51. Except as otherwise indicated, material in this section is based on Fred R. Harris, *Deadlock or Decision: The U.S. Senate and the Rise of National Politics*, pp. 202–236.

52. Howard E. Shuman, *Politics and the Budget: The Struggle between the President and the Congress* (Englewood Cliffs, N.J.: Prentice-Hall, 1988), p. 103.

53. Concerning the provisions of the Act, see Howard E. Shuman, *Politics and the Budget: The Struggle between the President and the Congress,* pp. 217–244.

54. See Howard E. Shuman, *Politics and the Budget: The Struggle between the President and the Congress,* p. 243.

55. Secretary of the Treasury Donald Regan told reporters at the time that "you cannot get inflation under control without having high interest rates." See "Reagan Says U.S. Will Adhere to Tough Monetary Policy," *Washington Post* (June 14, 1981).

56. Information concerning the history, provisions, and operation of the Gramm-Rudman-Hollings Balanced Budget and Emergency Deficit Control Act of 1985 is taken from Howard E. Shuman, *Politics and the Budget: The Struggle between the President and the Congress,* pp. 280–292; Lance T. LeLoup, *Budgetary Politics,* 4th ed. (Brunswick, Ohio: King's Court Communications, 1988), p. 153; and Joseph White and Aaron Wildavsky, *The Deficit and the Public Interest: The Response for Responsible Budgeting in the 1980s* (Berkeley: University of California Press, 1989), pp. 439–467, 506–529.

57. Then-U.S. Senator Gary Hart (D., Colo.), quoted in Fred R. Harris, "Deficits, Debt—and Gramm-Rudman," in Fred R. Harris, ed., *Readings on the Body Politic* (Glenview, Ill.: Scott, Foresman, 1987), p. 498.

58. For a history of the Bush budget summit and the facts surrounding it, see Fred R. Harris, *Deadlock or Decision: The U.S. Senate and the Rise of National Politics,* pp. 191–202.

59. Concerning the Clinton budget battle of 1993, see George Hager and David S. Cloud, "Democrats Tie Their Fate to Clinton's Budget Bill," *Congressional Quarterly Weekly Report* (August 7, 1993), pp. 2122–2129.

60. See George Hager, "A Process Packed with Power," *Congressional Quarterly Weekly Report* (June 5, 1993), p. 1414.

61. Personal interview by the author with Senator Johnston, Washington, D.C., September 28, 1988.

62. Personal interview by the author with Senator Domenici, Washington, D.C., September 16, 1988.

63. See Janet Hook, "Senators Offer Their Changes to Committees, Procedures," pp. 3030–3031; and Janet Hook and Beth Donovan, "Reform Panel Mirrors Issues Rather Than Mends Them," *Congressional Quarterly Weekly Report* (November 20, 1993), pp. 3171–3172.

EPILOGUE

1. Edward V. Schneier and Bertram Gross, *Congress Today* (New York: St. Martin's Press, 1993), p. 509.

2. See Richard L. Berke, "Politicians Find That Scandal's Touch Leaves an Indelible Stain," *New York Times* (October 4, 1993), p. A3.

3. See Michael Wines, "In Senate Streamline Plan, Powerful Would Be Less So," *New York Times* (November 5, 1993), p. A9; Editorial, "A Good Start on Overhauling Congress," *New York Times* (November 8, 1993), p. A14; and Janet Hook and Beth Donovan, "Reform Panel Mirrors Issues Rather Than Mends Them," *Congressional Quarterly Weekly Report* (November 20, 1993), pp. 3171–3172.

4. Barbara Hinckley, *Stability and Change in Congress*, 4th ed. (New York: Harper and Row, 1988), pp. 1, 13.

5. Samuel C. Patterson, "Congress the Peculiar Institution," in David C. Kozak and John D. Macartney, eds., *Congress and Public Policy: A Source Book of Documents and Readings,* 2nd ed. (Chicago: Dorsey Press, 1987), pp. 474–476.

6. Edward V. Schneier and Bertram Gross, *Congress Today,* p. 512.

Index

Medical perk, 35
Mexico, term limits in, 56
Mitchell, George, 103–4, 117
Money magazine, 11, 12, 29
Monroney, A. S. Mike, 38
Montoya, Benjamin F., 21
Morris, Governeur, 56
Moseley-Braun, Carol, 35
Moynihan, Daniel Patrick, 39
Murray, Patty, 61

Nader, Ralph, 16, 19, 26
Name recognition, as incumbent
  advantage, 66, 68
Nationalization of American society,
  67–68
National Law Journal, 99
Navy, Office of Attending Physician,
  35
Nepotism, 60
Neustadt, Richard, 94
New Deal, 2, 38
New Mexico State University, 31
New York Times, 6, 18, 35, 58
New York Times/CBS News poll, 7
Nickles, Don, 1, 122, 123
"Nightline," 11, 40, 48
Nixon, Richard, 6, 13, 61, 130
North American Free Trade
  Agreement, 100
Nunn, Sam, 96

Obey, David, 116, 118
Obey Commission, 43
Office of House Sergeant at Arms, 36
Office of Personnel Management, staff
  size in, 41
Office of Technology Assessment, 6,
  41
Official Secrets Act (Britain), 23
Oleszek, Walter, 100
Ombudsman function, 26, 69
Ornstein, Norman, 13, 33, 34, 35
Oversight function, 12

Packwood, Robert, 59, 137
Parker, Glenn, 5, 79, 81, 82, 84, 93
Parker, John, 99
Parliamentary system, 13, 23–24, 38
Patronage, 32
Patterson, Samuel C., 6, 82, 83, 84,
  93, 142–43
Pay. *See* Salaries, congressional
Pearson, Drew, 60
Peck, Richard, 31
Pension benefits, 31
Perot, Ross, 79
Pinckney, Charles, 16
Political Action Committees (PACs),
  73, 74, 75, 139
Political parties
  in Congress, 103–4, 105–7,
    114–15, 140
  decline in loyalty to, 67–68, 102
  and divided government, 102–3,
    140
  filibuster, 114–15
  homogeneity of, 104–5, 106
  ideological realignment of, 104,
    140
  and individualistic power model,
    91
  nominations of, 101–2
Polsby, Nelson, 6–7, 26, 29–30, 33,
  57, 57–58, 62–63, 113–14
Pomper, Gerald, 105
Postal Revenue and Federal Salary
  Act of 1967, 18–19
Postal Service, staff size in, 41
Poverty, 82
Powell v. McCormack, 51
Presidency
  approval ratings of, 84–85
  presidental-congressional conflict,
    93–101, 140
  strong, 2–3, 6
Press. *See* Media coverage
Proxmire, William, 5, 61
Public Citizen organization, 22